Food
for
Thought

About the Book:

This collection of daily meditations provides insight and encouragement for compulsive overeaters. *Food For Thought* is an inspirational guide used by members of Overeaters Anonymous and other self-help groups in their program of abstinence. Each meditation addresses the steps and concerns that can help recovering overeaters begin to benefit from a physically, emotionally, and spiritually balanced life.

Food
for
Thought

Daily Meditations

for Dieters and Overeaters

Harper/Hazelden

ISBN: 0-86683-503-2

Printed in the United States of America

5   4   3   2   1

Table of Contents

Good News

There is good news for those of us who over-eat compulsively. We do not have to be trapped by our appetites. We do not have to carry a load of unnecessary fat. We can have a new life.

Others have become free and are standing by, ready to show us the way. The more OA meetings we attend, the more we learn. The more phone calls we make, the more encouragement and support we are given in our fight to break old, self-destructive patterns of thinking and acting. The more we rely on the Power greater than ourselves, the stronger we become.

Learning to live a new life requires time and patience. The good news is that change is possible. Others have done it. So can you.

Lord, make me willing to change.

Help!

When we hit bottom and are ready to swallow our pride, help is available. When we admit that by ourselves we are powerless, a Higher Power takes over. Most of us have tried for years to control what we eat by ourselves. Often it seems that the harder we try, the more miserably we fail. We despair. When we are truly desperate and ask for help, OA can help us.

We have proven that we cannot solve our problem alone. A diet is not enough. We need a program that fills our emotional and spiritual needs as well as our physical ones.

Step by step and day by day we can learn to live without overeating. We will gradually become convinced that no amount of physical food will ever satisfy our emotional and spiritual hunger. The Higher Power which infuses each OA group becomes our lifesaver and our nourishment.

God, save me from myself.

Responding

Many of us find it difficult to accept the OA program at the beginning. Many of us cannot believe or are afraid to believe the good news at first. All we need to start is the desire to stop eating compulsively.

If we will be open to the program, we will find that it gradually unfolds. What we do not understand at the beginning becomes clear as we become ready to accept it. We shall never achieve perfection, but we can make progress every day.

When we are willing to grow and to change, God can work His miracles. OA is filled with members whose stories attest to the Power that has changed their lives.

I open myself to Your power, Lord.

Three Meals a Day

For most of us, abstinence from compulsive overeating means three measured meals a day with nothing in between. Before we joined OA, we often ate one enormous meal, all day long. Through this program, we find the discipline to eat according to our needs rather than our self-destructive cravings.

Unless a doctor has told us differently, we do not need more than three meals a day. As we practice this pattern, we re-train our overgrown appetites and learn to function in the real world. We can eat with our families instead of secretly snacking and bingeing.

We plan our three meals for the day, write them down, and report them to our food sponsor. Then, instead of nibbling here and there and thinking about food all day, we can forget about eating except when it is time for a planned, measured meal. As we acquire disciplined eating habits, we find that other areas of our lives become more ordered and productive. Freed from the bondage of self-will and impulse, we are guided by the sure hand of our Higher Power.

I am grateful for the order and sanity which OA has brought into my life.

Less Food, More Energy

When we have used excess food as a crutch for years, we think we need it to "keep up our energy." We have become especially dependent on the refined carbohydrates, sugar and flour, to give us a quick pick-up when we are tired.

The truth of the matter is that the pick-up, that sharp rise in blood sugar we got when we ate refined sugar and flour, was soon followed by an even sharper let-down. We ended up more tired than when we began! Excess food of any kind makes us groggy and lethargic.

When we eliminate the wrong kind of food and eat only the amount which our bodies need for optimum functioning, we are amazed at the supply of energy we suddenly have. Jobs which we have put off doing for years begin to get done. We feel good. Instead of spending unnecessary time for extra eating and digesting, we have that time to use in productive, enjoyable activity.

Try it and see.

Lord, strengthen my body to serve You.

Withdrawal

Eliminating all refined sugar and flour may seem difficult, if not impossible at the beginning. Making the decision to avoid these foods which trigger the craving for more and more is what opens the door to freedom. Freedom from the craving and freedom from fat.

We do not become free immediately. Some of us experience withdrawal discomfort, which is sometimes physical, sometimes psychological, and sometimes both. It is important to remember that the discomfort will pass, the craving will pass, and that if we remain abstinent, we will eventually feel much better. So much better that our bodies and our lives will seem new.

In order to walk into the world of freedom, we must go through the door of abstinence. We need not fear the pains of withdrawal. Growth is often painful. Many have gone before us and report that the eventual freedom is well worth the temporary suffering. Our Higher Power will give us the strength to endure and will never push us farther than we can go. When we are tempted to give in, a prayer and a phone call can save us.

Lead us into freedom, we pray.

Don't Take the First Compulsive Bite

OA says that if you don't take the first compulsive bite, you won't overeat. It is that first extra bite that gets us into trouble. The first bite may be as "harmless" as a piece of lettuce, but when eaten between meals and not as part of our daily plan, it invariably leads to another bite. And another, and another. And we have lost control. And there is no stopping.

It is the first compulsive bite that breaks abstinence. When we take it, we cheat ourselves and fall back into slavery to our appetites. To rationalize by saying that just a little deviation won't make any difference is like saying that someone is just a little bit pregnant.

All we have to give up is the first compulsive bite. Then we do not have to worry about the rest of them. Simple. Once we decide not to take the first one, our problem is solved. Abstinence is a lifeboat. It is possible to stay afloat in the lifeboat as long as we do not jump out by taking the first compulsive bite.

Thank you, Lord, for the saving gift of abstinence.

The Bottom Line

For everything worthwhile in life, there is a price to pay. The price is the bottom line. There is no free lunch. While we have learned that we cannot overcome compulsive eating without the support of our Higher Power and the OA group, we also know that OA is not a free ride to ideal weight maintenance. Each of us must look at the bottom line.

The price of freedom from compulsive overeating is the avoidance of all personal binge foods. It is the discipline of measured meals every day. We cannot have a new life of freedom from compulsion if we continue to cling to our old excesses. We cannot be free and overeat at the same time. We must be willing to pay the price.

As we move along each day in abstinence, we form new habits and we become accustomed to living without extra, unnecessary food. We begin to change in positive, constructive ways. One day at a time, in small installments, we pay the price of our new growth and progress. What we gain is infinitely more than worth the cost!

May I be willing to pay the price today.

Use the Telephone

When we join OA, we discover that we are not alone. We become part of a large network of individuals who share a common problem, compulsive overeating, and who gain strength and support from each other. The telephone is our lifeline. A phone conversation is a mini-meeting, and most of us find that we need several each day.

It is suggested that we make at least three phone calls every day, in addition to calling our food sponsor. We call in times of temptation and difficulty, and we also call when we have good news to share. A phone call may be a means of preventing problems later in the day or it may be simply a gesture of friendship and fellowship —keeping in touch.

Whatever the reason, the person called is helped as much as the caller. The telephone call is a reminder that none of us is alone, that we have a program which sustains us, and that together we shall succeed.

May I not be too proud or too shy or too busy to use the telephone.

Decision

Someone has said that the hardest part of the OA program is making the decision to follow it. You can do just about anything once you make up your mind to do it! But the decision has to be firm and it must be the kind of commitment which involves our deepest self.

Many of us who are compulsive overeaters have spent our lives looking for an easier way to lose weight. We feel that there should be a magic solution somewhere which will enable us to eat our cake and be thin at the same time. Our first reaction to the OA program is often one of dismay. It seems so drastic, and we protest that there must be an easier way.

The OA program is not easy. Life is not easy. Rather than solving the problems and difficulties in our lives, overeating multiplies them. We in OA have been offered a new way of life. Each of us decides every day—and many times every day—whether or not we will choose the new life.

May I decide to follow the program today.

No Amount Is Enough

For the compulsive overeater, one extra bite is too much and a thousand are not enough. No matter how much we eat, we are never "satisfied." We think we remember a time when a small extra treat made us feel completely satisfied and content, and we try desperately to recapture that sensation.

The more we eat, the worse we feel. Now, rather than satisfying us, the one extra, compulsive bite triggers an insatiable craving which drives us to consume enormous quantities of unnecessary food. Sometimes we stuff ourselves until we are exhausted, physically ill, or have run out of things to eat, but we are still not satisfied.

The more we eat, the more we want to eat. Each excess increases an already-out-of-control appetite. Since no amount will ever be enough to produce the kind of satisfaction we seek, our only hope is to abstain from the first extra, compulsive bite. Honestly following a food plan and eliminating all excesses and binge foods will eventually bring our runaway appetites under control. Conscientiously working the steps of the OA program will day by day bring us the emotional and spiritual satisfactions which we can never acquire from food.

Lord, show me how to work for true satisfaction.

Gratitude

I am grateful to have found OA. Without it, I would still be floundering in despair. I would still be alone, without understanding friends, without purpose, and without hope.

I am grateful to be abstaining just for today. I do not have to worry about tomorrow, because if I live well today, tomorrow will take care of itself.

I am grateful for a new life, for new strength growing out of old weakness.

When I am full of gratitude, there is no room left for anger, envy, fear, or hatred. Nor is there room for pride, since when I am grateful I am humbly aware of my dependence on my Higher Power. Being filled with gratitude is ever so much better than being filled with food!

May I gratefully abstain today and every day.

Overeating is Hell

When we fall into the trap of compulsive overeating, it is as though we are driven by some malevolent, diabolical force against which we are powerless. We know with our minds that we should stop eating, but by ourselves we cannot. A binge may start out pleasantly enough—just a taste here and there—but it eventually becomes torture.

Because we know what we are doing to ourselves, we feel guilty while we are bingeing. We hate ourselves because we cannot stop. The more we eat, the more uncomfortable we become physically and mentally. Clothes constrict and we are stuffed and bloated. Our minds begin to race along old, negative and irrational tracks. Anyone who gets in our way can be the object of our anger. We lose control, we are separated from our Higher Power, and we are in Hell.

Let us not forget every day that the first compulsive bite opens the gates of Hell.

Lord, deliver me from the Hell of overeating.

Willing To Go To Any Lengths

To achieve success in this program, we are willing to go to any lengths. We want to stop eating compulsively more than anything else. We are willing to take the steps which led to success for hundreds of others who have gone before us.

When we put abstinence first in our lives, then we are willing to experience periods of hunger and craving as our appetites and our bodies adjust to the new food plan. We are willing to eat according to need, not greed.

In times of stress and difficulty, we are willing to go to any lengths to stay on our program. This may involve going to extra meetings, making more phone calls, spending more time reading the literature and meditating. Whatever it takes to keep us abstinent is what we are willing to do.

Most important, we are willing to turn our lives over to the care of God as each of us understands Him. As we let ourselves be led hour by hour and day by day, our lives fall into place, and we are given inner joy and serenity.

I pray that I may always be willing.

Slips

Each time we give in to our giant appetite and go off the program, it is just as hard to get back on as when we first began. If we forget that we are compulsive overeaters and think that we can handle a little extra food like a "normal" person, we are deceiving ourselves. For us, one extra bite invariably leads to another, and we begin to slide downhill back into despair.

The longer we wait to get back on abstinence, the harder it becomes. If we slip, we sometimes feel that since we haven't been perfect we might as well go ahead and eat a lot, since we have blown our food plan anyway. When we do this, we punish ourselves.

If a slip occurs, we need to put it behind us. It is over and done. We cannot undo it, but we can at this moment stop eating and start abstaining again. We do not need to wait until another day. Every moment we have the choice of abstaining or overeating. Which do you choose right now?

May I choose to abstain now and always.

Act Your Way into Right Thinking

The OA program is one of action. For years, many of us have tried to analyze why we overate. The fact is that no amount of thinking will change our habits. To change, we must act.

We act by writing down a food plan, by picking up the telephone and calling a food sponsor, by going to a meeting. We act by buying the kind of food we need for our program. We act by planning our day so that we spend as little time as possible in the kitchen during those periods when we are likely to be tempted. We act by walking away from food which is not on our plan.

As we work the Twelve Steps, we take actions which result in concrete character changes. As we take the right action, our thinking changes and right thoughts come. But first we must act. What actions shall I take today?

Lord, direct my actions.

All We Have Is Now

We can only live now, this moment. We cannot erase the mistakes we made yesterday or bring back the good times we had. We cannot know what tomorrow will require of us nor can we insure future security and happiness. Now is what we have, and now is everything.

We can follow our food plan now. We can abstain this moment. We can deal with the problems which confront us today as best we can, trusting God to guide us. We can be in touch with our Higher Power only in the present.

As we focus on the present moment, we live it deeper, and we derive a satisfaction that we did not know when we were regretting the past and worrying about the future. Whatever happens, now is all I can manage and all I need.

Thank you, Lord, for this present moment.

Abstain or Overeat

For the compulsive overeater, there is always one primary choice to be made. Will I abstain or will I overeat? For us, there is nothing in between. If we have hundreds of pounds to lose or if we have reached and are maintaining our goal weight, the choice is still the same. It is the key decision we make many, many times each day.

We are free at each moment to choose which we will do. There is no magic which will make us abstain, and there is no force which can compel us to swallow food we do not need. The choice is ours alone.

No one graduates from OA. There is no point at which one can say, "This is it. I've got it made now." We are always aware of the fact that we are compulsive overeaters and are always one bite away from a binge. When we remember that abstaining or overeating is our primary choice, then other decisions become easier. To abstain is to choose life. To overeat is to choose death.

May I maintain constant awareness of my primary choice.

Be Not Anxious

If we are conscientiously working the OA program, we may leave the results to our Higher Power. To worry is to insult God. When we admit that we are powerless over food and that our lives have become unmanageable, we can then ask for and receive strength and power beyond ourselves. When we turn our will and our lives over to the care of God as we understand Him, we are free to live without anxiety.

At first, we are awkward. We turn over our problems and anxieties one minute and take them back the next. We forget that the Twelve-Step program has worked for countless other compulsive people—alcoholics and drug addicts as well as overeaters. Doubting God's strength, we fall back on our own weakness, and the result is trouble.

Through our contacts with OA members, we can see lives changed and people made new in body, mind, and spirit. These examples are convincing testimony to the efficiency of our Higher Power. The more we trust His will for us, the more He is able to work miracles in our lives.

Take my anxieties, Lord. I pray that Thy will may be done.

Avoiding Binge Foods

Most compulsive overeaters react to refined sugar and flour the way an alcoholic reacts to alcohol. One bite and we sooner or later go on a binge. We find it impossible to eat a controlled amount of food which contains refined sugar or flour, and we inevitably end up with a hangover from our excesses.

Many of us have other binge foods as well. We have learned from sad experience that it is easier to avoid these foods entirely than to try to eat them in reasonable amounts. We have to be rigorously honest with ourselves in order to determine which food plan is best for each of us as an individual.

No food is worth the anguish of a binge. Once we accept this, we can accept the necessity of abstaining from personal binge foods. Abstinence means freedom from the obsession with food and from the compulsion to overeat. Freedom to live without overeating is the reward we gain when we avoid the foods which trigger our compulsion.

May I realize that avoiding binge foods is a small price to pay for freedom.

Service

We compulsive overeaters have often spent our lifetimes being most concerned with getting, taking in, and consuming. Nourishing ourselves is necessary, but it is also necessary that we give. To stay alive, one must breathe out as well as in.

As we recover, we become stronger each day and better able to serve others. When we stop eating compulsively, we are amazed at the amount of time and energy we have available for useful activities. For one thing, we feel much better physically, since we are eating the amount and type of food which our bodies need for optimum functioning. For another, we become stronger emotionally and spiritually as we work the Twelve Steps.

Each day, we can be open to opportunities to serve our OA groups, families, and friends. As we give out more and take in less, we gain new satisfaction and self-respect.

Show me where I may serve, Lord.

There Is No Such Thing As "Have To"

The serenity and insight which we gain from this program help us realize that we do not *have to* do anything. There is always a choice. We may even choose not to live.

Our lives are gifts from our Higher Power, and the choice of what to do with them is ours. We can continue to overeat and watch our illness get progressively worse. We can isolate ourselves from other people and console ourselves with food. We can do as little as possible each day just in order to survive.

We do not have to follow the program; we also do not have to overeat. We do not have to turn our lives over to God; we also do not have to continue to bear the burden of self and self-will. It is a proven fact of experience for countless people that the most satisfying thing to do with the life given to each of us is to give it back to our Higher Power to use as He wills.

Thank You for my freedom, Lord.

Working the Steps

The OA program operates on three levels. Abstaining from compulsive overeating takes care of the physical aspect of our disease. For our emotional and spiritual health, we need to work the Twelve Steps.

In each of us, there is a need and desire to grow spiritually. At first, we may not acknowledge this need, but as our physical illness improves and our emotions begin to stabilize, we become aware of inner urgings and promptings that can come only from our Higher Power. If we set aside time each day to listen to this inner voice, we facilitate our spiritual growth.

Working the Steps requires that we be as honest as possible with ourselves at each stage of our development. A program sponsor who has walked the way before us is an invaluable aid. Above all, we must desire to grow. We have spent much of our lives over-growing physically. Now is the time to catch up emotionally and spiritually. If we make a sincere beginning, our Higher Power will lead us through each Step as we become ready to take it.

Lead me, Lord, and bless my work.

Humility

It is the suffering we experience as a result of overeating compulsively which eventually makes us humble enough to admit that we are powerless over food. Until we have the necessary humility, recovery is impossible. As long as we think we can successfully control and direct our lives by ourselves, we shall continue to fail.

Some of us hit bottom sooner than others. If we are lucky, we can see where the disease is leading us and what the inevitable result will be if we do not find help from a source outside ourselves. Whether we hit a high bottom or a low bottom, when we finally reach it the only way to go is up. When we are humble enough to seek help by turning over our will, we shall find the help we need.

Maintaining an attitude of humility is essential for our recovery. If we allow ourselves to fall into the trap of pride and egotism, we are headed for a slip. Understanding our weakness and dependence on God is the beginning of strength.

May I be granted humility.

Sharpening Our Tools

What we do each day is not as important as how we do it. If we are abstaining, working the program, and staying in touch with the Higher Power, then whatever we do during the day will go as it should.

When we get careless and sloppy with abstinence, neglect to use the tools of OA recovery, forget the Twelve Steps, then we may expect trouble. When we are out of touch with our Higher Power and our OA friends, then nothing seems to go as it should.

If you feel yourself becoming careless, then make that neglected phone call, read and re-read the literature, go to a meeting today. Listen within yourself for the quiet voice God uses to give you enthusiasm and direction.

We may each become God's tool if we keep ourselves in good working order through this program.

Make me an effective tool to do Your will.

Planning

There is a saying in our group to the effect that if we fail to plan, we plan to fail. If we do not have a food plan each day, we leave ourselves vulnerable to the attack of impulse and old habit.

Most of us find that we need to write down our three measured meals. Many of us continue to call them in to a food sponsor, even after the initial twenty-one days of abstinence. We can then go about the activities of the day without worrying about what we will eat. We become free to live without being obsessed with food.

Our pride often balks at the thought of calling another person and asking for help. We do not like to be committed to an eating plan. Let's remember that we tried to go it alone our own way, and that old way did not work. Let's be willing to try a new way that *has* worked for hundreds of OA members who are now at normal weight.

By Thy Grace, Lord, may I follow my food plan today.

Enough Is a Feast

The frantic search for more and more has characterized many of our lives. We believed that if only we had more money, more clothes, more sex, more food, more things—we would be happy and satisfied.

The more we consume, the more miserable we become. No amount of material things will satisfy our emotional and spiritual hunger. We learn to know our Higher Power, and we learn that He satisfies our need, not our greed. He feeds our hearts and our spirits with the abundance of His love, and when we are strengthened spiritually, physical control is possible.

Our measured food plan fills our bodily needs. The measured amount is enough. We accept it and become comfortable with it. More than that, we learn the truth of the ancient Zen saying that "Enough is a feast."

May I be content with enough instead of grasping for more.

Blessed Are the Hungry

When we are sated and overly full of food, there is no room left for the spirit. We feel like taking a nap, rather than working productively or playing enjoyably. During our overeating careers, how many hours have we wasted in bed, sleeping off the effects of a binge?

To eat no more than is necessary is to maintain our minds and bodies in a state of alertness and readiness for action. To say no to the sugars and starches which throw our blood sugar out of balance is to keep our energy level on an even keel.

As we lose excess weight and get rid of debilitating fat, we will probably experience some periods of hunger. There is nothing wrong with being hungry. Often it is when we are hungry that we are most humble and ready to listen to our Higher Power.

To accept physical hunger with serenity is to be spiritually strong.

I pray that my hunger may bring me closer to You, Lord.

Love Has No Calories

Moving through the Twelve Steps develops new ability to love. When pride and guilt are reduced, we can relate more genuinely to those we care about. OA gives us tools which we may use to escape the prison of self.

Our false defenses begin to crumble. As we learn to accept and love ourselves by the grace of God, we can reach out to others and give to them. Overeating destroys us; loving makes us strong. Growing in the program, we love more and give more. In return, we are given new joy and satisfaction.

Loving more may begin with the simple act of writing down the phone number of a fellow OA member and calling sometime during the week. It may mean taking five minutes to fully concentrate on what a child or a friend is trying to say. Food is no substitute for interpersonal relationships. We need to nurture the ones we have and build new ones as we become less dependent on eating and more committed to loving.

Teach me Your love, dear God.

Eat Less, Enjoy More

Before we joined OA, we were eating more and enjoying it less. The more we ate, the more fat we had to lug around, and the harder it was to do anything, much less enjoy doing it. Feeling stuffed and guilty, we often did not even enjoy what it was that we were eating.

When our bodies are not overloaded with too much food and fat, we have energy for new activities. Our minds are sharper when they are not drugged with refined carbohydrates. Our emotions are more serene and positive when we are not full of despair and self-hatred.

Freed from the terrible compulsion to eat more and more, we have time and energy to spend learning a new sport, reading a story to a child, writing a poem. Whatever we choose to do, we enjoy it more when we are not overeating.

When we abstain, we feel good about ourselves. When we feel good about ourselves, we feel good about life.

May I understand that for me, less food means more enjoyment.

Don't Be a Garbage Can

A garbage can is round and unprotesting as it accepts the leftovers which are stuffed into it. How many times have you treated yourself as a garbage can? As we stood up at the sink scraping what was left on the plates into ourselves, we rationalized that we just couldn't bear to waste good food. Why did we not remember the harm we were doing to our own bodies? "Is not the body more than food?" Certainly, it is more than a garbage can.

One way to eliminate waste is to prepare only what is needed for the meal. Sometimes we compulsive overeaters catch ourselves unconsciously overestimating quantities just so there will be something left to tempt us! Another way to avoid throwing out useable food is to keep a bowl in the refrigerator or freezer for scraps which can later be made into soup. We all know how to store complete servings for later use. It is the little bits here and there that get us into trouble.

If there is nothing that can be done with what is left in the bottom of the pan, then throw it away. Better to waste a small amount of food than to break abstinence, which is the most important thing in our lives.

Teach me to value my body more than food.

Learning

In this program, we never stop learning. It takes time to absorb the OA way of life. Some of us start with great enthusiasm, expecting perfection all at once. When we do not achieve it, we are sometimes tempted to give up and go back to the old, self-destructive way of eating the wrong kinds of food in the wrong amounts.

One of the most important things we learn in OA is patience with ourselves. We seek progress, not perfection. We work for it one step at a time, one day at a time. Our Higher Power accepts us and loves us as we are right now, today. By turning our lives over to Him and humbly asking for guidance, we become receptive to His teaching.

As we grow—slowly—we learn from our mistakes even more than from our successes. We are willing to be again as little children, and we are willing to accept suggestions and help from those who have had more experience and time in the program. We do not have to continue to make the same mistakes over and over again. We can learn the new way of life if we will walk into it patiently and slowly.

Open my body, mind, and heart to Your teaching, Lord.

Giving Thanks

I am a grateful compulsive overeater, abstaining just for today. I am thankful for my life, for the chance to grow and solve problems and love and enjoy what is beautiful. I give thanks for the insights which have come out of struggle and despair.

I am thankful for OA. Without it, I would still be isolated in a hopeless attempt to control overeating my way, by myself. I give thanks for the serenity and joy which increase daily as I follow the OA program. I give thanks for the love and support which come to me from fellow members.

Especially, I am thankful for abstinence. By choosing and accepting this gift, I enter a new world of freedom. No longer am I driven by compulsion. I give thanks for the work and play and love which abstinence makes possible.

Accept my thanks.

Food Is Not the Only Problem

The longer we are in OA, the more we realize that it is not only food which is our problem, but life. Our eating problem is also a living problem. As we maintain abstinence from compulsive overeating, our way of living changes.

Many of us have lived too much for ourselves and by ourselves. It is our egocentricity which has been our undoing. We have accepted no authority higher than our own whim and impulse, and we have been angry and depressed when people and events did not follow our preferences. Eating was an area in which we exerted our omnipotence, and appetite was our god.

When we are willing to acknowledge our dependency upon a Power greater than ourselves and when we become committed to abstinence from compulsive overeating, our living is put in order. When we eat right, we live right.

Order my living so that I may eat to serve You.

Don't Relax!

It requires extra effort to maintain abstinence during a particularly difficult time when we are especially tempted. Entertaining guests, visiting family, coping with a crisis—there are some times when it seems to take every ounce of strength we have to stay abstinent.

When the crisis has passed, we breathe a sigh of relief and are grateful that life is back to normal. This, for many of us, is the danger point. Having made it through the difficult situation, we may feel that we are now safe and can let down our guard. We may even feel that we deserve a reward for having said no to temptation.

Let's remember that the best reward is continued abstinence. There is no time when we are safe from compulsive overeating. We are always one bite away from a binge. We may never relax vigilance over our thoughts and actions.

When we are weary, let's remember that the strength we need comes not from ourselves but from our Higher Power. Let's recharge our batteries with prayer, meditation, and contact with other OA members.

Sustain me, Lord, when I am tempted to give up.

Slumps

Most of us go through periods in our lives when nothing seems interesting, when our motivation and enthusiasm have deserted us. We feel dull and bored and depressed. Whether the slump lasts for an afternoon or for a month or for a year, the compulsive overeater tends to turn to food as a way out. For us, food has been exciting, and eating often used to be the most pleasurable activity we could imagine.

As most of us know all too well, eating is not a permanent solution to boredom. We may get a temporary high from food, but we invariably eat too much and end up feeling infinitely worse than before we started. Boredom is better than a binge. Food does not motivate nor does it generate enthusiasm. Overeating has just the opposite effect.

Joining OA does not insure that we will never again experience boredom or have the blahs. What it does provide is a program of action to which we may turn when we are in a slump. Going to meetings, making phone calls, reading the literature, working the Steps—these are concrete actions we can take.

We have tried food and found that it eventually made things worse. Now let's try the OA program.

Give me grace to act.

The Power of Love

Love is the best motivation. When we are plugged in to our Higher Power, we are plugged in to love. It flows through us like a current, energizing our sluggish hearts and minds.

As we work the Steps of this program, we are given increased ability to love. By turning over our lives and our wills, we become receptive to the love which surrounds and sustains us. By taking inventory and being ready to have our character defects removed, we are able to get rid of old ways of thinking and acting which have been blocking out love.

We cannot produce love for others by ourselves, but we can receive it from our Higher Power. We can even receive love for people we don't particularly like.

Love gives energy for action and directs its course.

May I grow in Love.

Abstinence is Freedom

In the beginning, when we first practice abstinence, we may look at it as restriction, limitation, or denial. We don't like the word, we don't like giving up our favorite foods, we don't like measuring and weighing and writing down menus. We sometimes decide to abstain grudgingly, considering it punishment for past indulgences and bitter medicine for our disease.

Let's remember that what we are giving up is fat, lethargy, and the uncontrolled craving for more and more. Not to abstain is to remain a slave to compulsive overeating. Before OA, we were not free. We were prisoners of our compulsion.

Abstinence is not negative denial. It is positive freedom from the obsession with food and the debilitating effects of overeating. Through abstinence we become free to live active, interesting, satisfying lives. We are able to work and love and serve and enjoy in ways which were unknown to us before.

When we choose to abstain, we choose freedom.

Thank you, Lord, for freedom.

Small Decisions

We live this program one day at a time, one meal at a time. Throughout each day, we make many small decisions one at a time. We may often be tempted to take a tiny extra bite, to estimate a portion on the generous side rather than measuring it exactly, to include a problem food in our menu plan.

Each time we decide not to take the tiny extra bite, each time we weigh and measure exactly, each time we decide to avoid the problem food, we become stronger. The next wise decision becomes easier to make.

One wrong decision does not have to ruin an entire day. None of us is perfect. We can learn to accept the fact of a mistake and move on to the next decision which needs to be made. We can let our Higher Power total up our score and be the judge of how well we work the program. Our job is to work it, and at every moment we are free to decide wisely.

I pray for wisdom to make the right decisions.

You Are Not Alone

In the past, you may have fought a lonely battle with your inability to control your eating and the resultant weight problem. You may have thought that you were the only person who did such crazy, sneaky things in order to stuff yourself with food you did not need but could not stop eating. You may have lied to others about what you ate, and you may also have lied to yourself.

Family and friends probably tried to help. Despite the best intentions, it is difficult for one who is not a compulsive overeater to fully understand and help one who is.

In OA, you have been given a mutual support system. You have found people who understand you because they are like you. We all have the same problem, and together we are strong enough to solve it. Let's use the help that the OA fellowship gives us and gain strength from the greater strength of the group.

May I contribute to the warmth and support of the OA fellowship.

Write Before You Eat

When you are tempted to grab an extra bite, stop and make contact with another OA member. If you cannot bring yourself to make the call, or if you make it and still want to eat, then try writing.

Before you take the bite, write down exactly how you are feeling, what you think the extra food will do for you, what the likely result will be, and how you will feel an hour later. It is a good idea to keep a pad of paper handy in the kitchen; you can grab a pencil instead of food.

Often the process of writing down exactly how you are feeling will reveal the hidden emotions which are masquerading as hunger and a desire to eat. You may discover that you are angry, or fearful, or lonely. Write the feelings and write the consequences of eating because of them.

Grant me insight, Lord, and self-understanding.

Simplicity

Someone has said that God is simple; it is we who cause the complications. The more we are able to simplify our lives, the more effective we become.

A simple eating plan frees us from being preoccupied with food. We decide what we will have for our three measured meals, we may call the plan in to a sponsor, and then we can forget about food. We are free to concentrate on the jobs and activities of the day. In contrast, how muddled and messy our lives were when we were bingeing!

Turning our will and our life over to our Higher Power frees us from preoccupation with self. Rather than trying to figure out complicated methods of getting things to go our way, we are free to live each day as God gives it to us, trusting His will.

As we grow in this program, may we grow in simplicity.

Acceptance

When we have given our lives back to our Higher Power, we gradually learn to accept what happens to us as part of His plan. Most of us made a mess of trying to run our own lives. We are amazed at how much better things go when we acknowledge that the Power greater than ourselves is in control.

Every experience, the bad one as well as the good one, becomes an opportunity to learn and to serve. We may not like what it is that we are given to do or to feel on a particular day, but we learn to accept it as necessary for our growth. We can look back and see that we have learned even more from our failures than from our successes.

When we accept our lives and ourselves as part of God's creation, we are open to the work of His spirit and His love. Then positive change and growth become possible.

Teach me to accept Your will.

Being Honest

During our compulsive overeating careers, many of us have been dishonest with others about what we were eating. Some of us have been closet eaters and some of us have stolen food. Most of us have eaten more when we were alone than when we were with other people.

We have almost surely been dishonest with ourselves, too. How many times have we promised ourselves to stick to a diet, only to find ourselves cheating a short time later? We tell ourselves that one small bite won't make any difference, when deep down we know that we intend to eat many more bites than one.

When we take inventory, and as our insights are sharpened, we may discover other areas besides eating where we have not been honest with ourselves.

The OA program gives us a chance to practice rigorous honesty, especially with ourselves. The light from our Higher Power will gradually clear away our confusion and darkness.

May I not be afraid to know the truth.

Satisfaction

When we were overeating, we thought mainly about trying to satisfy ourselves. The more we ate, the more we wanted to eat. The more we ate, the less satisfied we were. We finally realized that satisfaction was not to be found by consuming more and more food.

When we stopped overeating, we suddenly had much more time and energy available for constructive activities. We began to contribute more to our families, our jobs, our recreation. We found new areas where we could be of service to others.

Because OA has given us so much, we in turn are able to share with our groups. As we give to others, we receive self-satisfaction as a by-product. This is a much more powerful satisfaction than we ever found in the refrigerator!

For each of us, serving and contributing to the best of our abilities means abstaining. Without abstinence, we can never be satisfied.

Thank You for opportunities to give and for the satisfaction of abstinence.

Beginnings

Each day is a new start. Each moment is a beginning.

We do not have to wait until Monday to get back on the program or clean a closet or tackle a difficult report. We do not have to wait until tomorrow morning, either. Now is the moment to stop eating, to make a phone call, to begin whatever project we have been putting off.

There is no way we can change what we did five minutes ago, nor can we predict what will happen half an hour from now. We can only deal with now.

By doing what needs to be done right now, we make the most of each present moment. As long as we are alive, we are always free to begin again. Instead of following an old, worn-out habit, make a fresh start this moment on the rest of your life.

Give me grace, Lord, to begin again.

Meetings

We have proved that we cannot control our eating alone. Through OA, we have found a way that works, provided we work the program. If we become careless about attending meetings, we are thrown back on our own weakness.

It is the OA meeting which gives us the hope and enthusiasm we need to continue in the program. The sharing and fellowship of the group provides strength and encouragement. In times of difficulty, most of us find that the more meetings we attend, the better able we are to cope.

When we don't feel like going to a meeting, it may be because our old overeating habit is trying to surface. We are never cured of our disease and we never outgrow our need for the strength, fellowship, and love we receive from OA meetings.

I give thanks for OA.

Forgiving Ourselves

We would like to be perfect, and when we make mistakes, it is hard to forgive ourselves. If we eat something not on our food plan, the resulting anger at our weakness may escalate a small slip into a full-scale binge. When we are under pressure and act foolishly or say something unkind to someone close to us, we may punish ourselves by eating or by sinking into a black mood.

In order to get back on a positive track, we need to forgive ourselves and put the mistake behind us. It does no good to dwell on our weakness and rehash what we should have done and say "if only. . . ."

In OA, we become humble enough to admit that we will never be perfect. We strive for progress. Forgiving ourselves is necessary so that we may make a positive change.

As You forgive, may I forgive.

Setting Priorities

One of our slogans is "first things first." We cannot have or do everything; we must set our priorities and choose what means the most to us.

Each of us needs to spend quiet time searching the inner self to determine which people, which activities, which tasks are most important. The results may surprise us. We may find that we are spending too much time with someone we really do not enjoy, preparing complicated meals which no one needs, working at a job which we dislike in order to make more money to buy more things. Do we really need the things? Do they enrich our lives or are they merely impressive?

Because I am a compulsive overeater, abstinence is the most important thing in my life. Without it, I do not enjoy other people, I do not like myself, I do not work well. If abstinence does not come first, everything else suffers.

May I remember that abstinence is my number one priority.

Responsibility for Whom?

Before we came to OA, some of us felt responsible for seeing that others did what we thought they should do. By the time we took the Fourth Step, and often long before, we began to realize how manipulative we had tried to be. We may not have thought we could run the whole world, but we sometimes felt that we should maintain control over our little corner, at least.

Through this program, we are learning that we can only be responsible for ourselves. We cannot change anyone else. We can only work on ourselves. No matter how good our advice is, it is useful to someone else only if that person desires and requests it.

Learning that we are responsible to our Higher Power for ourselves alone lifts a heavy weight from our weak shoulders. We stop trying to decide what others should do and how they will react to what we do. We do the best we can, seeking guidance and direction from God, and then we leave the results to Him.

Show me my area of responsibility, Lord.

A Selfish Program

We call our program a selfish one. It is something which we want more than anything else, not only for weight loss but also for peace of mind. We do not join OA to please anyone else; our primary purpose is to do what is best for ourselves.

Starting the program where we are, we take the aspects of it which apply to each current situation. We give to and share with our group, but we also remember that the best thing we can do for any other compulsive overeater is to practice our own abstinence.

We have found that putting ourselves down does no good, either to ourselves or to anyone else. If for someone else we do something which we sincerely believe is wrong for us, then our resentment is bound to come out sooner or later.

When we were overeating compulsively, we often tried to hold down our resentment with food. Instead of honestly facing anger and hostility, we tried to make it go away by eating.

The OA program gives us a better way to deal with negative emotions, and for selfish reasons we need this program!

May I not be afraid to recognize my needs.

Serenity

Serenity comes when we are tuned in to our Higher Power. Serenity enables us to take external circumstances in stride, even the most difficult ones. Serenity is a gift which we are each free to receive daily.

Turning our will and our lives over to God as we understand Him encourages serenity. Staying in contact with our Higher Power as we go about our daily activities produces serenity. Practicing abstinence from compulsive overeating maintains serenity.

In meeting after meeting, we hear people testify to the change that has come over them since they began the OA program. Circumstances which once would have sent them into a tailspin and into the refrigerator are now manageable. By the grace of God, they have been granted the serenity to accept the things they cannot change.

May I grow in serenity.

Spirituality

Ours is a program for living spiritually as well as physically. We have found that without daily spiritual nourishment we feel an emptiness which no amount of material things can fill. We have also found that when we were overeating and were physically glutted, we were less receptive to spiritual food.

In Step Eleven, we seek to improve our conscious contact with God as we understand Him. We do this through daily prayer and meditation. Our contact with our Higher Power is most effective and satisfying when we are carrying out the physical part of the program by maintaining abstinence.

When we came into OA, most of us wanted to eat less in order to lose weight. As we grow through the Twelve Steps, we gradually learn that eating less physical food enables us to make more spiritual progress. The rewards of working the OA program are far greater than we had imagined! The spiritual food which we receive from our Higher Power begins to satisfy the emptiness which we had foolishly tried to fill with excess calories. Not only do we maintain abstinence in order to control our weight, but we also maintain it in order to grow in spirituality.

May I remember to seek spiritual food.

Dependency

In the past, we used excess food as a crutch, and we developed a false dependency on it. We turned to unnecessary food to calm us down, cheer us up, and in order to avoid facing our problems. As a cure-all, food let us down. Rather than solving our problems, overeating multiplied them.

As human beings, there are many times when we are weak and dependent. If we say we can go it alone, we are whistling in the dark and deluding ourselves. We need to rely on a Power greater than ourselves, but food is not that Power. What we need to find is the Power strong enough to sustain our dependency.

Accepting the fact that we are dependent, that we cannot manage our lives by ourselves—this is the beginning of recovery. We need to be humble, open, and willing to be led by those who have replaced their false dependency on food with a healthy dependency on God.

Lord, may I not be too proud to be dependent on You.

Values

What do I value most? What is number one in my life? What is at the center?

When I was overeating, I was the center. I was the biggest thing in my universe, and all else revolved around me. A frightening state of affairs, since egotism does not bring peace of mind or security. Self was most important to me, and that egotism was my downfall. When I fell off my high horse and hit bottom, I had nowhere to go except to something outside of myself.

As we compulsive overeaters take Step Two and come to believe that a Power greater than ourselves can restore us to sanity, then we begin to shift the center of our consciousness from ourselves to God. This is our only hope. As long as our weak selves are at the center, we cannot make real progress, either in controlling our addiction or in living useful lives.

When we hit bottom, we are humbled. When we are humbled, we are able to perceive and acknowledge that God is primary and that abstinence is our most important task. Values are sorted out and order brings inner peace and security.

You, Lord, are the center of my life.

A New Place

After a slip, we do not go back and start again in the same place where we were before. Through the experience of making a mistake, we have reached a new place. Out of error, we can gain new knowledge and insight.

Often we find that wrong thinking got us into trouble. Perhaps we fell back into the old perception of ourself as the center of the universe. Perhaps we forgot to turn over whatever was troubling us and instead began to overeat. Perhaps we tried to depend on our own inadequate strength to get us through the day. Undoubtedly, we forgot that abstinence is the most important thing in our lives without exception.

Whatever the mistake, we can profit from it by growing in understanding and insight. We can mark a pitfall to be avoided in the future. We start again a few steps farther ahead, in a new place.

May I not be discouraged by mistakes.

Eating Slowly

We compulsive overeaters are inclined to devour our meals in a great rush. Mealtime often finds us anxious and tense, and sometimes we are just plain greedy! While others at the table are interested in conversation and socializing, we may be narrowly focused on food and preoccupied with trying to satisfy a ravenous appetite.

We need to break out of our self-centeredness. Rather than being completely absorbed with satisfying our own appetite (which we can never do), we can learn to focus some of our attention on the concerns of those around us. When we eat more slowly, we have more time for others and we feel less deprived. Our enjoyment, of both the company and the food, is greatly increased.

Even when we eat a meal alone, we should remember that we do not receive all of our nourishment from physical food. When we eat more slowly, we become more relaxed and refreshed both physically and spiritually. When we are aware of our Higher Power and thankful for all of His blessings, the meal is more satisfying.

Help me to slow down and appreciate Your gifts.

No Standing Still

Life is movement, and to be alive is to change. There is no standing still. Either we are making progress in the control of our disease, or we are getting worse.

Progress forward is an upward climb. To look back with longing at a time which in retrospect seems easier, or to think about the so-called pleasure we once got from food, is to invite disaster. We have long passed the point of being satisfied with a small amount of uncontrolled eating. Now, a small amount will inevitably become a large amount and instead of pleasure, we will eventually feel much physical and emotional pain.

If we are making progress, let's keep at it and not be deluded into going backwards. If we are losing control and slipping, let's recognize that we are on a downward course and that our disease is getting worse. Let's stop rationalizing and making excuses. Right now we can turn around and start climbing.

May I keep climbing.

Conserving Resources

In this fight against compulsive overeating, we need all the strength we can muster. We can learn to conserve our energy for what is important, rather than wasting it on non-essential activities.

An extra hour of sleep may do more for our program than an hour spent reading a novel or watching television. We have to guard against compulsive overactivity as well as overeating. Often, we tend to push too hard to complete something which can just as well wait until tomorrow. If we are tired, we are less able to resist temptation.

Choosing the foods which will provide us with necessary proteins, vitamins, and minerals is a vital part of maintaining energy. To take care of our bodies is to nurture the most valuable physical resource we have.

Conserving our resources often means saying no to people and activities which drain them unnecessarily. Only we ourselves, with the guidance of our Higher Power, can decide how best to use the strength and energy we have.

Teach me to conserve the resources You have given me.

Other People's Problems

Sometimes we wear ourselves out trying to solve another person's problem. Is this not perhaps a form of egotism? We feel that somehow we should have all the answers and be able to find a solution to every problem, especially when someone close to us is in trouble.

We may be sympathetic and supportive and helpful, but we cannot play the role of God in another person's life. Even our children must learn from their mistakes, just as we continue to learn from our own. If I trust my Higher Power to lead and direct me, then surely He will also direct my family and friends.

The best thing I can do for anyone else is to maintain my own sanity and sobriety. If I eat over a problem—whether it is mine or yours or ours—then I am less able to deal with it.

There are times when no solution seems forthcoming, when an unfortunate or tragic circumstance must be accepted and lived with in the best manner possible. We may not be able to change the circumstance, but we can be sure that God will give us the strength to deal with it.

Grant me the serenity to accept the things I cannot change.

Changing

As we lose weight, we adjust to a new self. Part of the body we had is disappearing, and this can be frightening. As our physical appearance changes, others may react to us differently. Along with the physical changes go new attitudes and expectations. Though for years we may have wished to be rid of the fat, when it actually begins to go we may fear the change.

What is new and unknown is often frightening. We may have used food and fat to retreat from uncomfortable situations. We may have spent so much time eating that there was little left for anything else. We may have expected all our troubles to vanish with the excess pounds. Now we can no longer hide behind fat or kill time with food, and our troubles may very well still be with us. What do we do?

It takes courage to change, to become a new person. We may decide at age forty to learn to play tennis. That takes lots of courage. New activities, new attitudes, changes in relationships with others—all require courage.

Change is frightening, but it is also an adventure. We are not alone. We have OA. Others have gone through the same changes and can reassure us, one step at a time.

May I not be afraid to change.

Precision

For the success of our program, many of us have found that it is important to be precise when we weigh and measure our food. It has been our experience that carelessness and sloppiness lead to cheating and bingeing.

An extra spoonful or ounce here and there may not seem important, but it can soon become an extra portion. Then it is easy to think that since we have not followed our plan exactly, we might as well go ahead and really indulge.

There are circumstances when weighing and measuring is impossible; then we estimate as best we can. However, for most of us, most of the time, precise measurements are possible and are a valuable aid in maintaining abstinence. Each time we put back the extra spoonful of carrots and cut away the extra ounce of meat, we are stronger. It is always the first extra bite that is the downfall of the compulsive overeater. If we are careful and precise in our measurements, we will not take it.

Accuracy is honesty.

Make me honest with myself, Lord.

Doing What Feels Good

Doing anything as long as it feels good is a trap. We like to eat for the sheer sensual pleasure of the experience, and we would like to continue long after our need for nourishment has been met. Once our appetites are out of control, we cannot stop, not even when the pleasure has turned to pain.

Unbridled, uncontrolled sensuality will destroy us. Rational knowledge of when to stop is not enough. We may know with our minds that we should not be eating, but still be unable to stop the action of our bodies. If we are unable to control our sensuality with our minds, then how is it to be done?

OA members testify that there is One who has all power, including the power to enlighten our darkness and prevent our self-destruction. Through daily contact with this Higher Power, we develop spiritual strength which will control and direct our physical drives so that they do not control and destroy us.

Take my sensuality, Lord, and control it.

Old Tapes

In the recesses of our minds, each of us has old tapes stored away which tend to be played over and over again. These tapes may have been recorded so long ago that they have little if anything to do with our present situation.

The tapes which are recordings of positive thoughts and experiences can be helpful when replayed. Unfortunately, we each possess many tapes which are negative and self-destructive. They include resentments, fears, and hates. When one of these negative tapes begins to play, we may find ourselves opening the refrigerator or going out to buy food which we should not have. Often the tapes continue to play while we are eating.

Taking an inventory each day makes us increasingly aware of our negative emotions: anger, envy, irrational anxiety. Admitting mistakes and making amends relieves us of the guilt associated with our character defects.

By giving our lives to God and staying in contact with Him, we are able to turn off the negative tapes. We receive new thoughts and positive feelings: hope, faith, love.

I pray that my thoughts and feelings may be purified.

Living Now

When we were eating compulsively, we left the here and now. We escaped into fantasy, and we were often unaware of how much we were eating. By some strange mental quirk, we were able to forget that we should have been burning up our excess fat, not adding more.

God is now. To make contact with Him is to bring ourselves in touch with what is real. When we first came to OA, we may have had doubts, if not downright disbelief, about the reality of God, but concrete experience has convinced most of us that a Higher Power is indeed in control.

In order to be rid of the mental obsession which drives us to the insane behavior of compulsive overeating, we practice being constantly tuned in to our Higher Power. He can restore us to sanity and keep us living in the present. By giving Him our past resentments and future fears, we become free to focus on the here and now. Without resentment and fear, we can see the beauty of the present moment.

Lord, keep me living in the here and now.

Accepting Abstinence

Abstinence is not so much something we achieve as it is a gift from our Higher Power. It is given to us constantly, from the time we wake up in the morning through every minute of the day.

If we think of abstinence as something we have to acquire through great effort, we will be afraid that we will fail. We will think of weeks and months and years stretching ahead of us and say, "I'll never make it."

Abstinence is given to us now, each day, and all we need to do is accept it. It is not something we do only in order to lose a certain number of pounds. By abstaining, we will lose the pounds, but when we are at our desired weight we continue to maintain abstinence. Abstinence is our freedom from compulsive overeating and the gift of new life.

Thank you, Lord, for abstinence.

"Normal" Eating

The idea that we will one day be able to eat spontaneously, like normal people, is a delusion. We compulsive overeaters tend to think that once we lose our excess pounds, we can go back to "normal" eating. Not so.

It is our experience that once a compulsive overeater, always a compulsive overeater. There is no way we will ever be able to eat spontaneously without eventually getting into trouble. When we reach our desired weight, we continue to eat three measured meals a day with nothing in between, and we continue to avoid entirely our personal binge foods.

When we accept our permanent need to abstain, when we accept the fact that we can never return to what we thought was normal eating, then we can stop making irrational attempts at experimentation which always fail. By accepting our disease and learning to live with it, we become sane and free. We see that our new eating plan is really very normal. It was the old compulsive overeating habit which was abnormal in the extreme.

Thank you, Lord, for sanity.

No Ultimate "ah"

When we were overeating, we sought an ultimate experience of satisfaction from food. No matter what kind of food we ate, or how much, we never found that moment of satisfaction, that ultimate "ah". It was always just ahead, in the next bite.

Have we finally realized that the ultimate "ah" which we looked for in food does not exist? No matter what we eat, or how much, it will always elude us. Whatever we are looking for—happiness, success, peace, fulfillment—it is not to be found in the refrigerator.

We do not promise that working the OA program will bring instant gratification or constant happiness. What we do know is that through the Twelve Steps we are given positive experiences which we did not have before OA. We are happier, more successful, more at peace, and more fulfilled than we ever were before we found this program.

By realizing that food holds no ultimate "ah", we can stop destroying ourselves by chasing a rainbow which does not exist.

May I stop searching for happiness where it is not to be found.

Fellowship

Compulsive overeating is a lonely activity. The more we eat, the more we isolate ourselves from other people and the more alienated and different we feel. We need people, but we do not like ourselves, and we fear that others will reject us.

What a relief to find a group of other people with the same problems and feelings! We are accepted, understood, and loved. We find that we are not so different after all.

The OA fellowship exudes a sense of warmth and support. It is a safe place to put aside masks and express honest feelings. There is healing and strength. Meetings and retreats have given many of us a deeper experience of belonging than we have found anywhere else. We are all accepted as we are and where we are in our personal development.

No one tells us what to do in OA. Through the fellowship, we learn what has worked for others and we find relief from our loneliness.

Bless our fellowship, Lord.

Sharing

In our fellowship, we share our troubles and we share our joys—our faults as well as our assets. We will be accepted and understood, because we are with people who are like us. We may seem very different on the surface, but underneath we are all amazingly alike.

Someone has said, "I can only know that much of myself which I have had the courage to confide to you." As we reveal ourselves to others, they act as mirrors so that we may see and understand who we are.

All of us have hidden fears and buried guilts. Before we joined OA, we had no place to go with these negative emotions, and so we turned to unnecessary food. Instead of rationally facing our worries and our hurts, we ate. Even when we were happy, we found it easier to eat than to express our joy to someone else.

Sharing our thoughts, feelings, and experiences with other people shows us who we are and helps us to accept ourselves. Those with whom we share also benefit.

Grant me courage and trust, so that I may share.

Nourishment or Drug?

During our overeating days, many of us used food as an all-purpose drug. It was a pep pill when we were depressed and a tranquilizer when we were uptight. We turned especially to refined carbohydrates as uppers and downers. As a result, we spent most of our time either artificially stimulated or lethargic.

When we stop using food as a drug and eat only what our bodies need for proper nourishment, we experience emotions which had been buried by overeating. We feel anxiety, fear, and anger. We also feel joy, enthusiasm, and love. We are alive instead of doped up.

We need to express and share our emotions, and in OA we find people who will help us do that. We no longer have to bury our true feelings with food. As we learn to rely on our Higher Power for support in the little things that come up as well as the big ones, then we are able to face the day without a drug.

By abstaining, we learn who we really are and what we really feel.

May I not be afraid to live without a drug.

No More Diets

OA is not another diet club. Abstinence is not something we go on for a while, until we achieve a desired weight goal, and then go off. We are through with diets. In the past, they may have worked for a time, but sooner or later we became bored with them, quit, and regained the weight we had lost.

OA is a program of recovery. We discover that what we eat is not the most important thing in our lives. Each day we plan what is necessary for the nourishment of our bodies, and then we are free to forget about food and go on with our living.

Instead of following a diet for a certain length of time, we maintain abstinence from compulsive overeating every day of our lives so that we may feel good and function effectively. We work the program, live the Twelve Steps, and enjoy each day as never before. We are recovering.

Thank You for the gift of recovery.

Power

Our group is infused with a Power that changes lives, the Power of love and fellowship. So many of us can attest to the daily miracles that God has performed and is performing as we live this program. The changes and miracles may happen slowly, and our spiritual growth may be gradual; nevertheless, the Power is real.

As we become aware of this Power, we see how weak and unnecessary were the false supports we had relied on in the past. We probably sought strength in material possessions, personal achievement, social status. These supports all failed us, and we ate to hide our weakness.

Now that we have experienced the Power of the OA fellowship, we no longer have to rely on false supports. We can grow in the program and in closer contact with the One who creates and sustains us.

May I rely more completely on You.

Keep Planning

Maintaining our abstinence means that we continue to plan our three measured meals each day. To leave them to chance is to invite trouble, since compulsive overeaters do not learn how to eat spontaneously, no matter how long they try.

Planning means that we have the food we need available when we need it. We make decisions about what we will eat when we are rested and strong, not when we are in a rush, over-tired, or over-hungry.

Preparing meals ahead for busy days, shopping for food after a meal rather than before, remembering to allow time for defrosting—there are many ways to make it easy to follow a food plan. When we are convinced that abstinence is the most important thing in our lives, we are able to find ways to maintain it no matter how difficult the circumstances.

Help me to remember to plan.

Difficult Times

When we have hard things to do, we especially need our abstinence. We know from experience that maintaining it is the only way we can feel good and cope effectively.

Formerly, we turned to food to strengthen us and prop us up during difficult times. We invariably ate too much and were less able to manage the troublesome situation. Food then became an escape, and we sometimes ended up doing nothing at all about a problem, since we had eaten ourselves into oblivion.

We know now that instead of strengthening us, extra food incapacitates us. No matter how difficult the situation we face, we know that eating unnecessary food will eventually make it worse.

We have come to believe that whatever happens, our Higher Power will give us the strength we need if we will rely on Him.

May I rely on You, Lord, instead of food.

Vulnerability

When we stop doping ourselves with unnecessary food, we become vulnerable. We have been using extra food as a defense against our feelings. Without it, fears and anxieties surface and new energies are released. Instead of retreating into the refrigerator, we can learn day by day how to live with our exposed selves.

Making an overture of friendship to someone we would like to know better involves the risk of rejection. Saying no to a family member when a request conflicts with our program may make us feel guilty. Asking for help when we need it means admitting our weakness. Exposing our needs destroys our facade of self-sufficiency.

To be vulnerable requires courage, but only as we are able to live without the defense of overeating are we able to grow emotionally and spiritually. When we stop turning to food to cover up our feelings and needs, we are able to be more open with other people. We are nourished by them and by the Higher Power who allays our fears and directs our new energies.

May I not fear being vulnerable.

A New World

Being abstinent puts us into a new world. Instead of trying to cheat ourselves and get away with it, we learn to be straight with ourselves and others. Instead of escaping problems, we learn to face them honestly. Instead of despair, we feel self-respect and a developing self-confidence.

As we get rid of our obsession with food, we get in touch with our feelings and abilities so that we are able to function calmly and efficiently.

All of this does not happen overnight. We take the Twelve Steps under the guidance of a program sponsor. We work our program every day. We continue to use the telephone and go to meetings so that we may learn from other members.

Above all, we maintain contact with our Higher Power, since it is by His grace that we have entered this new world.

Thank You, Lord, for leading me to a new world.

Strength

In the past, we relied on our own strength to get us where we thought we wanted to go. We were afraid, since deep down we knew how weak and undependable our own strength really was.

When we turn our lives over, we no longer have to go it alone. We have tapped the limitless reservoir of strength provided by our Higher Power, and when we are operating under His guidance we feel confident. What we could not do ourselves can be done when we admit our weakness and ask for help.

Through working the OA program and through closer contact with our Higher Power, we may find that we are going in a new direction. The things we thought we wanted may turn out to be unnecessary, and we may have new goals. Wherever our journey leads, we will have the strength we need, since it does not come from ourselves but from a Power greater than ourselves.

I need Your strength, Lord.

Peeling Off Layers

As we work our program, we peel off layers of old, worn-out thoughts and habits. OA gives us a place to share old hurts and fears so that we are able to get rid of them. Our OA friends accept us and give us the benefit of their experience. With their help, we are able to leave the old layers behind and move ahead.

We never stop learning and growing. When we are ready to accept it, our Higher Power reveals just as much truth to us as we can assimilate. He directs our progress through the Steps of this program as we are prepared to take them.

If we are sincere in our efforts, the right help will come when we need it. It may come through another member, a piece of literature, a new insight, or even a difficult experience. Peeling off and discarding worn-out layers of ourselves is hard work and is often painful. But when we look back and see how we have grown, the satisfaction more than outweighs the pain.

Guide me as I peel away and leave behind the useless thoughts and habits I have accumulated.

Letting Go

By admitting that we are unable to manage our own lives, we become ready to let a Higher Power take over. Before we can fully benefit from God's direction, we must let go completely of the idea that we are in control.

We say that we are grateful compulsive over-eaters, because if it had not been for our inability to control what we ate and the resulting turmoil in our lives, we might never have realized our need to "let go and let God."

When we turn our problems over to our Higher Power, we leave them with Him and move as He directs. If we take the problems back, we are like a child who has given his parent a broken toy to fix, but snatches it back before the parent can make the repair.

If we had been able to fix our problems ourselves, our way, we would not be in this program. Since we know we need help, let's be willing to let go and try God's way.

May I let go of my problems so that You may direct my life.

Abstinence Is a Way of Life

Each morning when we wake up, we give thanks for another day of abstinence. Our bodies feel good, function well, and look better. To go back to our old ways of eating compulsively would be to give up the new health and peace of mind which we have acquired through OA.

We do not want to go back. We are learning a new way of life, one that is infinitely preferable to our old ways. In order to maintain our abstinence and continue to make progress, we need a program. For most of us, this involves working the Twelve Steps each day.

Program sponsors can help us with this new way of life. Other OA members share their experience and tell us what has worked for them. Most of us find that we need the spiritual part of the program if we are to maintain our abstinence. Abstaining purely for weight control is usually not enough.

If we are to keep what OA has given us, we have to share it with others. We find that the more we give it away, the more progress we make with our own program.

To abstain is no sacrifice; it is growth and life.

I am grateful for this new life.

Awareness

To be aware is to be focused and alive. If we are truly alert to what is going on within and around us, we will never be bored. Through working the OA program, we develop greater awareness of ourselves, other people, and our Higher Power.

Sometimes this new awareness brings pain; we realize that we have been hurt and that we have hurt others. Through our daily inventories, we recognize shortcomings and mistakes which we may have ignored in the past. Often it is too late to undo all of the damage which has been done by our compulsive overeating and general self-centeredness.

Here is where we pray for acceptance of what we cannot change and courage to make amends where we can. It is then important to put what is past behind us and concentrate on being more aware now, today, so that we do not make the same mistakes again.

When we are not dulled by too much food and the wrong kinds of food, we are more perceptive and aware in every aspect of our lives. Our experiences are richer and we are better able to grow and change.

I pray for increasing awareness.

Action

Ours is a program of Action. It does no good to develop new awareness if we do not take appropriate new actions. When we become aware of the damage done by compulsive overeating and realize that OA has the answer to our problem, we take action by going to meetings, making phone calls, and working the steps. We follow a food plan and abstain from eating compulsively.

Taking inventory, admitting our mistakes, and making amends involves action. Our Higher Power gives us courage to change the things we can. He gives us the confidence to get involved in new activities, to be more assertive, to make new friends, to go back to school, to change jobs.

By abstaining from the type of eating that paralyzed us, we have strength and energy to do new things. One step at a time, we are led into action. Not to move according to the direction of God as we understand Him is to fall backwards and stagnate. Each positive action we take strengthens our recovery.

Direct my actions, Lord.

Living Day by Day

"Life by the mile is a trial; by the inch it's a cinch." In the past, we got into trouble when we thought we had to have our lives mapped out forever. That just did not work.

We need only deal with the problems and joys of today. If we try to see too far ahead, we lose touch with the reality of the here and now. The Lord lets us know what we need to know when we need to know it.

What seems impossible when looked at in total—writing a book, putting the children through college, abstaining for the rest of our lives—becomes manageable when worked at step by step, day by day.

So many of the things we worry about never happen. How much better it is to concentrate our energies on the real demands and challenges of today, insignificant as they may seem. When we turn our lives over to our Higher Power, we trust Him to manage the master plan and to direct us in the small details of living each day.

Show me, Lord, how to best live each day. I leave the years to You.

Cobwebs and Illusions

We compulsive overeaters react to refined sugar and starches as an alcoholic reacts to alcohol. When we were overeating, our thinking was foggy. The more we ate, the more confused we became. We often lived in a world of cobwebs and illusions and were unable to separate fact from fantasy.

This cloudy thinking caused all sorts of complications in our relationships with others and lowered our general level of efficiency. We found ourselves becoming very angry and irrational when events did not go our way. We often made life miserable for our families, taking out our anger on them. Sometimes we escaped into a world of fantasy where we would be omnipotent and where our every whim would be indulged.

When we came to OA and began to practice rigorous honesty, we discovered that in order to be honest we had to abstain from the kind of eating which confused our thinking. It is amazing how abstinence can clear away cobwebs and illusions!

Thank You, Lord, for sanity.

Finding Our Place

I did not create this world, nor did I create myself. I do not know what the outcome of my life will be, or even what will happen to me next week. If I try to manipulate reality and arrange circumstances to suit myself, I become frustrated and unhappy. I cannot control reality, but I can change myself to be more in harmony with it.

When I accept a food plan and follow it, I am slowly adjusting my body and my appetite to what is best for my health and well-being. I have tried the other way—adjusting my intake of food to the demands of my appetite—and the result is disaster and chaos in my life.

In OA, we follow a program which is sound and which has worked for thousands of compulsive overeaters like ourselves. We stop trying to make everything go according to our desires, and we start learning how to live in the real world. With the guidance of our Higher Power, we find our place.

I trust Your guidance.

Avoiding Trouble

Staying out of the kitchen as much as possible is a good way for the compulsive overeater to avoid trouble. If fast-food restaurants are a problem, then visit them as infrequently as you can, or keep away from them altogether.

With planning, we can arrange for the food we need without placing ourselves in situations of great temptation. If the family is having something not on our program, we can substitute a simple meal for ourselves which fits our food plan. Sometimes we may need to get out of the house entirely while a particular food is being served.

Whenever possible, we stay away from temptation. We strengthen our resolve and refresh our spirits by frequently making phone calls to other OA members, attending meetings, and reading the literature. As we progress in our program, we are bothered less and less by the foods which we have chosen to avoid. Our new way of eating and living is so much more satisfying than our old habits that we have no desire to jeopardize it.

Lead us away from temptation.

Slow Success

We say that there are no failures in OA, only slow successes. Some of us take longer than others to catch on to the program. It is important to keep trying, to continue to attend as many meetings as possible, and to refuse to become discouraged.

There are some of us who spent months and years experimenting before we were finally able to accept abstinence and stay with it. Sometimes we left the program for a time, until we realized how much we needed OA and came back to try again.

When we have accepted the program and maintained abstinence, yet found weight loss to be extremely slow, it is easy to become discouraged. It helps to remember that we are not only losing weight—however slowly—we are also learning a new way of life. Our spiritual and emotional growth in this program is even more rewarding than the eventual weight loss. By living each day as it comes and working the Twelve Steps, we achieve the serenity and confidence that make us satisfied with slow success.

May I be granted patience and persistence.

Simple Joys

When we came into OA, we may have thought that we needed many material possessions, power, security, and great admiration from other people in order to be happy. We may have spent a tremendous amount of effort trying to acquire these things. Perhaps we were apparently successful, and yet were miserable because of our inability to control our eating. No amount of material possessions, fame, or prestige can alleviate the pain of compulsive overeating.

Abstinence is simple. It does not require great wealth, talent, or intellectual ability. It is immediately available to all of us. When we abstain, we know the simple joy of waking up in the morning feeling good. We can live without fear of our next eating binge. We find that we enjoy our three simple meals a day much more than our former overindulgences.

Through OA, we can accept ourselves and others for what we are. We do not have to impress each other. Friendship and sharing increase our joy.

Thank You for the simple joys of abstinence.

Sanity

Once, a long time ago, I was able to eat a small amount of extra food between meals and then stop. I enjoyed it very much. Over the years, that small amount became more and more. Somewhere along the line, I crossed the boundary of rational eating and moved into an area of insane bingeing.

Now, when the old urge comes for a small amount of extra food, I need to remember that I am incapable of stopping after a reasonable amount. For me, the first compulsive bite is now the point of no return. Once I take it, I cross immediately into insanity.

How do I remember? I need protection against the arrogant, willful delusion that "This time I will be able to handle it; this time I will get away with cheating just a little bit." How can I protect myself?

Step One says that we are powerless over food. From sad experience, I know this to be a fact. Step Two says that we "came to believe that a power greater than ourselves could restore us to sanity." My protection comes from this Higher Power.

Keep me sane, Lord.

Came to Believe

Perhaps we have believed in a Higher Power all our lives, or perhaps we have been agnostic. In either case we have been unable to apply faith and belief to our greatest problem—compulsive overeating.

OA asks only that we be willing to believe and that we keep an open mind. As we hear the stories of members who have come to believe through the program, our own faith grows. As we experience God's grace, our belief increases.

Steps One, Two, and Three work together. Only by admitting that the problem has us defeated, that we are powerless—only then do we become open to a Higher Power. If there is no way that we can stop eating compulsively by our own strength, then we require a strength greater than our own. Others have found this strength in God, as He is understood by each individual. When we turn our will and our lives over to our Higher Power and practice the Twelve Steps every day, we apply our belief and faith. The belief may be very small and weak in the beginning, but like the mustard seed, it grows. Gradually, we become convinced of what we had known all along, but were afraid to believe.

Strengthen my belief, I pray.

Food Is Not God

Though we may not have admitted it, food was probably the most important thing in our lives when we were overeating. How many times did our relationships with family and friends suffer because of our slavery to our appetites? How often did we hurt those we loved by placing our craving above their needs?

Instead of loving God first, most of us loved food first. And it let us down. Rather than making us stronger, the excess food we consumed made us weaker. In place of happiness, overeating gave us increasing misery.

Whenever we put a material thing in the position of supreme importance in our lives, we are headed for trouble. It doesn't work. We are physical beings, but it is our spirituality which is of ultimate value. If we miss this aspect of our lives, we flounder without purpose or direction. The more we rely on a material thing such as food (or money or status or drugs), the more enslaved we become.

We find that when we put our relationship with our Higher Power first in our lives, then everything else, including food, falls into place.

May You always be first.

Trusting God

Most of us have spent a great amount of time and energy trying to order and arrange our own lives. We have searched frantically for something to hang on to which would solve our problems—a new diet, a new job, a new lover. Nothing has worked permanently. The harder we have tried to straighten ourselves out, the more our problems have defeated us.

When we came into the OA program, we were advised to "let go and let God." At first, this may have seemed to us to be a huge cop-out. The idea of passively waiting for a Higher Power to do for us what we could not do for ourselves was an insult to our pride and our illusions of self-sufficiency. We were afraid to let go.

Our Higher Power requires that we be willing to trust Him with our lives in order to receive His strength and direction. From our vantage point of limited knowledge, there is a risk involved in letting go. If we are willing to take this risk and if we have the courage to face our fear, we will eventually receive the peace and support which we so desperately need. Besides, what do we have to lose except our own weakness?

Grant me courage to trust You completely.

Resting

We compulsive overeaters often used food as a stimulant when we felt the need to be busy about something. Of course, food did not keep us stimulated for long, since we usually ate too much and ended up in a stupor.

With this program, we can be more in touch with how our bodies really feel. There are times when the craving for food may mask our fatigue, times when what we need is rest, not food. When we are tired and feel that we cannot continue with what we are doing, it is very possible that we need to rest rather than eat. A short nap can refresh us much more than unnecessary food.

True rest for our spirit as well as our body comes from our Higher Power. A period of meditation can lift us out of mental and emotional depression. Only a brief moment is required to take our attention away from the daily routine and let our consciousness be drawn to God. These frequent pauses during the day tap a vast storehouse of energy and power.

I rest in Your greatness, Lord.

Fears

Do you eat when you are afraid? Many of us do. When we were babies, being fed brought the safety of our mothers' arms. As adults, we sub-consciously give food a sort of magic ability to ward off real or imagined danger.

There are times when food may serve as a temporary tranquilizer, but overeating prevents us from facing what we fear and learning how to deal with it. Eating compulsively, moreover, usually produces a feeling of guilt and a fear of "getting caught." The fear that we will not be able to stop eating is added to the fear that prompted us to reach for food, and the more we eat, the greater our fears.

Many of our fears are groundless and irra-tional. Through contact with our Higher Power, we are given the sanity which causes them to disappear. Those fears that remain are often the result of the self-centeredness which prevents us from turning our lives completely over to God. When we give Him absolute control, we have nothing to fear.

May I love You enough to let go of my fears.

Giving Up Delusions

As we work the steps of the OA program, our new actions produce new thoughts. When we are ready, our Higher Power reveals new truths and gives us new insights.

Gradually, we give up old, deluded ways of thinking. We realize that we had put self at the center of the universe, and we see this to be a delusion. We may have secretly considered ourselves better than those around us. Once we honestly take inventory and face up to our defects, we can no longer believe this. Another common delusion is that material goals will bring us ultimate satisfaction. When we admit the pain we have caused ourselves and others by our insatiable cravings and demands for material things, we see that they are not the answer.

Most of us have harbored the delusion that one day we will be completely rid of the temptation to overeat, and that we will then be able to relax our efforts. It is our experience that continued effort is required to maintain abstinence and that only through daily dedication to the life of the spirit are we able to receive sanity, strength, and satisfaction from our Higher Power.

Take away my delusions, Lord, and show me Your truth.

Appetite

Appetite grows as it is fed. The more we eat, the more we want to eat. If we let any physical appetite take over—whether it is for food, sex, security, or whatever—we become its slave.

If we do not nurture our relationship with our Higher Power so that God is the ultimate authority for everything that we do and the object of our greatest desire, then we will be enslaved by one or more of our physical appetites. When God is perceived to be the greatest good and the source of all joy and satisfaction, then physical appetites fall into their proper place.

First we seek spiritual growth. Our primary desire is to do God's will for us, as He enables us to do it. When He is our Master, His love feeds our spiritual appetite and we begin to know the inner peace and satisfaction which the world cannot give.

May my desire be always for You.

The Enemy Within

Why do we self-destruct? The problem of evil has been with us ever since the serpent tempted Eve to eat the apple. We often feel at war internally, one self fighting another self.

There are forces that would have us abandon our program, and usually we find the temptation coming from within. We become careless, bored, lackadaisical in our efforts. Instead of disciplining ourselves to further spiritual growth, we rest on our oars and then wonder why we are drifting downstream!

There is nothing wrong with our bodily appetites except when we allow them to take control. Then they will destroy us. Sane, healthy living requires that we acknowledge our spiritual needs. When our Higher Power is in control, we work for emotional and spiritual growth as well as physical satisfaction. Instead of being divided internally, we are integrated. The enemy within is subdued in the only way possible—by God's power.

Defeat the enemy within me, Lord.

Retreats

OA retreats are a wonderful way to recharge our batteries and gain strength through sharing. Whether for a day or for a weekend, the retreat is an extremely effective tool for growth in our program.

If an organized retreat is not available when we need it, we can arrange our own personal retreat for a day or two. Choosing a day or a weekend when we can concentrate on our program may give us the boost we need when we are having difficulty. If a minimum of time is spent on necessary tasks, there will be many hours free for reading, writing, and meditating. We can plan our abstinent meals ahead of time so that they require as little preparation as possible.

A personal retreat may take place at home or, if there are many distractions and it is possible to leave for a day or two, we may go somewhere away from home where we can be quiet and reflect. Extra time spent in prayer and meditation yields enormous dividends, and we return with increased strength and perspective.

I seek the refreshment that comes from You.

Increasing Joy

Before we found OA, many of us felt depressed much of the time. The combination of too much food and too little inspiration was lethal. We existed and we did what we had to do, but there was a lack of deep joy in our lives.

When we get the poisons out of our systems which have been deposited by refined starches and sugars and by overeating in general, we feel one hundred percent better. As we get rid of the poisons in our minds and hearts, our joy increases.

Gradually we are relieved of the guilt of overeating. We are also relieved of envy, anger, fear—all of the negative emotions which have poisoned our hearts.

Deep joy can only come from the deepest part of ourselves. That is the place where we find and come to know our Higher Power.

Thank You, God, for increasing joy.

Deliverance

OA is here to say that compulsive overeaters have been delivered from compulsive overeating! We have found a way of eating that delivers us from fat and, even more important, we have found a way of living that delivers us from fear.

The price is high. We find that in order for the program to work, we need to give ourselves completely to it. We have proved over and over that half measures do not succeed. Unless we keep our will and our lives entirely in the hands of our Higher Power, we will fall back into the trap of compulsive overeating and compulsiveness in other areas.

Every day when we wake up, we give thanks for another day of abstinence, and we put ourselves under God's care and direction. We ask that we be guided in all our activities and that we may follow His will for us in all that we do. Then, whatever happens during the day, we accept it as part of God's plan, and we play our part as He directs us. The outcome and results belong to Him. We are delivered from self-centeredness and freed from compulsion.

We celebrate our deliverance.

Compulsive Means <u>My</u> Will

When I am compulsive about something, I "have to" have it or see that it is done. I am insisting on my will, my way. I forget that the world does not revolve around me.

Going against the laws of the universe inevitably brings trouble. I cannot willfully consume everything my uncontrolled appetite demands without hurting myself and others. I cannot arrange other peoples' lives to suit my time schedule. I cannot adjust the world to me; I can adjust myself to what is, to reality.

Giving up my selfish, egocentric desires is probably the most difficult task I have. "He who masters himself is greater than he who conquers a city." I cannot do it alone. Through the fellowship of OA, with the help of the program, and by the grace of my Higher Power, I seek to turn from my will to His will.

Thy will be done.

Greed

How many of us are killing ourselves with our own greed? In spite of all that we take in, we remain empty. Excessive consumption depresses our spirits even before it destroys our bodies.

Why are we so empty? Is it because we search for fulfillment in the wrong places? Do we expect permanent satisfaction from new clothes, more food, a bigger house? When the acquisition of these things fails to satisfy us for long, we then think we must go out and get more clothes, better food, a more elegant house.

Sometimes our greed arises out of fear, fear that we will not have enough. Gibran says, "What is fear of need but need itself? Is not dread of thirst when your well is full, the thirst that is unquenchable?" [1]

We are all children of a Father who satisfies our need but not our greed. To trust Him to abundantly supply all that we truly require is to give up fear as well as greed.

Take away my greed, Lord.

[1] Gibran, Kahlil. *The Prophet*. Alfred A. Knopf, 1954. p. 19.

Gluttony

In the Middle Ages, gluttony was considered one of the seven deadly sins. Now that sin has become an unpopular concept, we are inclined to overlook gluttony. It is still listed in the dictionary and defined as "eating to excess." Every compulsive overeater knows only too well what that means.

OA says that gluttony begins with one bite too much. When we give in to that first compulsive bite, we walk from the protection of our Higher Power into the snare of self-indulgence. Sometimes we are lucky enough to escape before the consequences are disastrous, but usually we are caught in our own trap.

There is no cure for gluttony, but we can stop practicing it. We can refuse to take the first extra bite. We can so strengthen our minds and hearts with the gifts of the Spirit that we do not need to eat to excess. The time we spend each day working the steps of our program is our insurance against gluttony.

By Thy grace, protect me from gluttony.

A Daily Reprieve

Through the grace of our Higher Power and by means of the OA program, we compulsive overeaters are given a daily reprieve from our disease. This reprieve, however, is dependent on our spiritual condition. If we do not stay in touch with our Higher Power and if we do not practice the OA principles each day, we lose the reprieve and fall into compulsive overeating.

Our program comes first; other concerns are secondary. OA is not something which we can tack on to our schedule when it is convenient. To be effective, it requires top priority. This does not mean that we spend all of our time involved in OA activities. It does mean that all of our activities are guided by spiritual principles.

Impossible? Only if we refuse to turn our lives over to our Higher Power. When He is in control, our work, recreation, and rest all come under His direction. We are spiritually in tune each day and safe from our disease.

Thank You for saving me from my disease today.

Helping Others

Twelfth Step work is essential in OA, since in order to keep the program ourselves we have to give it away. Each of us finds opportunities to share what we have received.

It is discouraging when someone we wish to help turns down the program. It is hard to know what to say or do when a friend who needs OA responds to our efforts with indifference or hostility. Sometimes, those we are trying to help take advantage of our time and patience. Often, we feel inadequate when we encounter a person with seemingly overwhelming and insoluble problems.

As we go about our Twelfth Step work, let's remember that the best way we can help someone else is by maintaining our own abstinence. Let's also remember to turn over our perplexities to our Higher Power. We do the best we can, according to the insight we are given at the time, and we leave the results to God.

Show me what to do for those I would help.

Easy Does It

Strain and struggle abound when we try to do everything ourselves, our way. We want positive change to occur immediately and expect miracles to happen according to our personal timetable. We sometimes feel that if our Higher Power is guiding us, we should be able to accomplish great and marvelous things constantly.

To remember "easy does it" is to humbly realize that we are not all-powerful and that God does not expect us to be all things to all people. Growth is slow, time belongs to God, and change will occur according to His plan. If we do the jobs we have been given for this 24-hour period, our Higher Power will take care of tomorrow.

How much more agreeable life is when we do not overextend ourselves but admit our weakness and trust God to take care of us. We do not shirk our share, but we do not try to carry the whole load. Only our Higher Power is strong enough to do that.

Take from our lives the strain and stress.

Caring

"Teach us to care and not to care. Teach us to sit still." [1]

We know that God cares for us and we try to give to those we love the care that He would have us give. But sometimes we become so caught up in our cares and concerns, whether they be for ourselves or for others, that we forget to listen to our Higher Power.

In order to work the spiritual part of the program, we need to spend time quietly by ourselves listening to the inner voice. Each day we need a period of time alone when we can get in touch with the center of our being.

When we are tuned in to our Higher Power, we are able to give to those we care for. Our concerns fall into proper perspective, and we are freed from selfish preoccupation. Our actions become more effective and our hearts are more open to the needs of those we love.

Teach us to care.

[1] Eliot, T. S. "Ash Wednesday."

Perseverance

We all go through periods when we seem to be standing still or slipping backwards. It is often difficult to stay with our food plan when weight loss slows or stops. We may become bored with the program if our understanding of it is superficial. There are many times when things do not go the way we would like, and we may be tempted to give up.

Let's remember where we began and how miserable we were before we found OA. If there are times when abstinence does not seem so great, let's remember how much worse the alternative is. We have been down in the depths of despair before, and we do not choose to go back there.

One day at a time, we can keep moving forward. Even when we see no signs of progress, we can know that our Higher Power is now in charge of our recovery and that His purposes never fail.

Lord, give us strength to persevere.

Social Situations

Many of us find it especially difficult to follow our food plan when we go to parties and eat with friends. We may feel deprived if we do not eat and drink what everyone else is eating and drinking. Sometimes we maintain our abstinence at the party and then go home and break it for some strange kind of emotional compensation.

The longer we live the OA program, the easier it becomes to deal with social situations. We begin to realize that the company is more important than the food and drink, and we discover that we can enjoy being with our friends regardless of what we are or are not consuming. We also become convinced that only by abstaining do we maintain our health and sanity, and we value these more than whatever refreshments are being served.

Because we are stronger now than we were before, we are less affected by the social pressure to do what everyone else is doing. We know who we are and how we can best live our own lives.

May I enjoy my friends more than food.

New Skills

When we stop eating compulsively, we get out of ruts that we may have been in for years. Our schedules change, since we spend less time eating. The confidence we gain encourages us to try new activities, and we discover skills we never knew we had.

Because we are no longer disgusted with ourselves, we get along better with those around us. As we learn to give up fear and self-centeredness, we find ourselves turning out better work and performing well in areas where before we had been weak.

Spiritual growth is the key to the new developments in all parts of our lives. We have become more closely connected to the source of creativity, so we are more alive. Others respond positively to our new sincerity and enthusiasm.

That we may continue to grow and learn gives us quiet satisfaction. For this, we are grateful to OA and our Higher Power.

Thank You, Lord, for newness of life.

Happiness

Happiness is rarely achieved by pursuing it. We compulsive overeaters used to think that food could make us happy, but we found that it could not. Many of us tried other substances, too, such as alcohol, drugs, or money. When these also failed us, we may have decided that only a perfect partner could make us happy. Alas, we soon discovered that there are no perfect individuals, only ordinary people with faults like our own.

So where does happiness fit in? At some point along the line, we abandon the frantic pursuit of an external object of happiness and begin to work on ourselves. As we go through the Twelve Steps, we become less self-centered and more focused on a Higher Power. As we are able to concentrate more on His will and less on our own, we find that periods of happiness come as a by-product. Paradoxically, when happiness is no longer our goal, we have more of it.

In You, there is joy.

Wisdom

The longer we live this Twelve-Step program, the more we realize that we do not have all the answers. Our finite knowledge is very limited, and we need all the help we can get.

Acknowledging our limitations and our powerlessness is the beginning of wisdom. Conceding that we cannot manage our own lives puts us in a position whereby we may humbly ask for the wisdom that comes from our Higher Power.

If we are to grow in wisdom and learn which things to accept and which to change, we need to conscientiously devote time each day to the OA program. We need to read and re-read the literature. We need to examine our motives and our deeds. We need to act according to the promptings of our Higher Power.

Wisdom is not acquired overnight. The more patient we are and the more humble, the better able we are to learn from the mistakes we make.

May I stay close to You, the source of wisdom.

Hungry or Bored?

When we ate compulsively, we often interpreted boredom to be hunger. When there seemed to be nothing else to do, we could always eat! Unstructured time may have made us anxious; we thought we could fill up with food and allay our anxieties.

To be egotistical and self-centered is to be bored. If we are always the center of our awareness, we will soon tire of ourselves, since none of us is all that fascinating. In order to escape boredom, we need to turn our attention outward and focus on something besides self.

When we give our lives to our Higher Power, we are making a commitment of service. We are asking that His will be done and that He use us as He sees fit. By relieving us of our obsession, God frees us from slavery to our appetites. If we are to remain free, we need to serve Him instead of ourselves. Day by day, He shows us our tasks and as we become absorbed in them, we lose our boredom along with our false hunger.

May I know the true nourishment of doing Your will.

Forgetting Food

Abstinence enables us to stop being preoccupied with food. We decide that we will have three meals a day with nothing in between, and we have a definite plan for those meals. Whenever cravings or thoughts of food begin to distract us, we put them out of our mind. We remember that food has proved to be a false friend, and we no longer permit it to control our life.

Through OA, we have found new interests and activities. We have friends to call when we are lonely or upset. When we are feeling shaky, we can go to a meeting. Perhaps our new energies have led to involvement in community activities, new jobs, hobbies and projects.

Each of us faces a certain amount of sluggishness and inertia when we decide to get involved in something new. It is easier to stay in the same old rut, since we often fear what is untried and unknown. Let us not permit apathy or anxiety to weaken our resolution. Escape into food and overeating is no longer an option.

Keep my thoughts on the new possibilities which You have opened for me.

Overcoming Sloth

Another of the seven deadly sins which we do not talk much about any more is sloth. Webster defines it as laziness or indolence. It is our experience that the more we eat, the lazier we become. We procrastinate, we do not feel like undertaking anything difficult, and we avoid movement as much as possible.

Abstinence puts our bodies into high gear. With proper nourishment and without an excess amount of food to digest, we feel alert and alive. We find ourselves requiring less sleep and fewer naps. Lifetime habits of laziness do not change immediately, but if we are willing to become more energetic, our Higher Power will provide the motivation.

Sometimes the thought of a large task looming ahead of us is overwhelming, and we feel that we will never be able to manage it. Here is where the willingness to take one step at a time can make the difference. If we will begin, God will keep us going when the task is part of His plan.

Deliver us from slothfulness.

Food Is No Cure-all

In spite of what we compulsive overeaters may have believed, food does not solve our emotional or spiritual problems. Food cannot fill our hearts with love, no matter how much we eat. Rather than erasing our difficulties with family, friends, and self, overeating multiplies them.

If our problem were that of not having enough to eat, food would be the solution. It is possible for us to be overweight and undernourished at the same time, if we are eating the wrong foods. For most of us, though, the difficulty is simply that we like to eat too much. The only cure-all for that problem is eating less!

The good news for compulsive overeaters is that a life of abstinence and control is possible. We do not have to be destroyed by our disease. When we recognize that we have been using food to do what only our Higher Power can do, we are on the way to recovery. Instead of turning to food to ease our aches and satisfy our cravings, we turn to God.

Thank You for being there for me.

Failure

If the OA program demanded perfection, then we would all be failures. Our goal is progress, not perfection, since none of us will ever be perfect.

It is said that the only time we fail in OA is when we do not try again. When we stumble or slip in our physical abstinence or in our emotional and spiritual life (and the three are always interrelated), the important thing is to pick ourselves up and keep going. We may lose battles here and there, but if we rely on our Higher Power, we will win the war.

None of us is free from temptation. Even when we abstain from compulsive overeating we may indulge in self-pity, envy, or anger. There is always the danger of pride and self-will. Perhaps it is through our failures that we become humble enough to seek and accept God's help. If we could manage by ourselves, we would have no need for a Higher Power. A failure is an opportunity to start again.

From failure, may I humbly learn to walk more closely with You.

Judge Not

When we have received the gift of abstinence and have gotten rid of excess weight, we sometimes tend to be very critical of those who have not yet succeeded with the physical part of the program. We may also be especially critical of those who obviously need the OA program, but who are not yet willing to try it.

Then there are some of us who resent those who come into the program with very little weight to lose or those who are of normal weight but nevertheless suffer from compulsive overeating.

Instead of worrying about other people and trying to pronounce judgement on their needs and efforts, it would be better to concentrate on our own progress. Only God understands completely where we are at a given moment, and only He can judge our sincerity and growth. We can help and encourage each other, but we are each responsible to our Higher Power.

To refrain from judging others is to stop trying to compare apples and oranges. We are each unique, and we grow according to our individual timetables.

May I not waste time and energy judging others.

Waiting and Acting

Do you seem to have spent much of your life waiting for something? Waiting for Santa Claus, waiting to grow up, waiting to get married, waiting for children, a better job, etc., etc. When we join OA, we wait for the time when we will be thin, thinking that surely then everything will be as we want it to be.

It is important that we begin to live more fully now, rather than projecting our satisfaction into an indefinite future. Rather than waiting for tomorrow, let's obey our inner voice today. Rather than reaching for another bite that we do not need, let's enjoy the measured meal that we have in front of us. Instead of waiting to be thin, let's become more active now, even if all we do is go for a walk around the block.

There are some things that require patient waiting. But there are other things which we need to make happen now by taking action.

Lord, grant me the wisdom to know when to wait and when to act.

We Are Insatiable

Those of us who overeat compulsively can never be satisfied with food, no matter how much we eat. As we work the program, we discover (if we had not known it before) that we are insatiable in other areas, too. No amount of anything satisfies us for long; we soon need more.

We are each created with a spiritual longing which is not filled by anything temporal. What St. Augustine said hundreds of years ago—that our hearts are restless until they find their rest in God—is equally true today. Spiritual food is required to satisfy our spiritual hunger. The fruits of this world are good in their proper place, but when we idolize them we sell ourselves short. Created things in and of themselves are not enough; our hearts can accept nothing less than communion with the Creator.

We are children of God, and the things of this world do not fully satisfy us.

May we find our true rest and satisfaction in You.

Commitment

Our commitment to OA is total. The program is not something we pick up and put down according to whim. Abstinence is not a diet that we go on and off as it pleases us. Perhaps a seeming inability to commit ourselves to anything permanently has been one of our problems in the past. If so, we are now all the more aware of the necessity for genuine, total commitment to this program.

Most of us tried just about everything else before we came to OA. We may even have tried OA previously and left, thinking that there must be an easier way. Now we are desperate because we know that there is no other way for us. Our recovery depends on our willingness to commit ourselves honestly to the OA program and to work it day by day to the very best of our ability.

When we are firmly committed to the Twelve Steps and the OA principles, we are able to apply them to all aspects of our daily lives with astonishing results.

Strengthen my commitment, Lord.

Accepting Normality

It is normal to eat three meals a day. As compulsive overeaters, we made ourselves exceptional by refusing to follow the usual pattern of meals. Instead, we wanted to follow the whims and demands of our irrational appetites. For some reason, what was good enough for others was not good enough for us—we had to have more.

Now that we have accepted a reasonable food plan, we can learn to eat normally. We do not need extra food. We know that our true strength and nourishment come from our Higher Power, not from an overload of calories.

When we stop overeating compulsively, we no longer need to feel guilty about our eating habits or different from those around us. We can accept the fact that we are normal people, not better than everyone else and not worse either. Like those around us, we have strengths and weaknesses, and we are making progress. It is a relief to accept normality.

May I keep a realistic perspective on myself.

Food Is Not Enough

Food is fine, as far as it goes, but it doesn't go far enough. We need our three meals a day, planned according to the requirements for healthy nutrition, but we do not live by food alone.

We need close contacts with friends. We need to be involved in productive work and stimulating activities. We need to serve in the areas where we are best qualified. We need to use our God-given talents and abilities rather than sitting on them. Especially, we need the spiritual qualities of faith, hope and love.

In the past, we may have given up on "religion." Through the OA program, we have found that our Higher Power did not give up on us. He has led us to this plan of recovery and is offering each of us the possibility of a richer, fuller life. God never intended us to be satisfied with physical food and material things. He daily offers us much more.

Fill my spirit, I pray.

Slow Down and Live

Many of us rush through our days as well as rush through our meals. Often we let ourselves get so busy that we do not enjoy what we are doing or what we are eating. We swallow life in great gulps instead of savouring it moment by moment.

Hurry and busyness are forms of self-will. Deluded by an exaggerated sense of our own importance, we deem it crucial to perform all tasks and activities according to our personal schedule. Impatient with traffic tie-ups, other people's slowness, or unavoidable delays, we make ourselves tense and miserable by our refusal to accept life as it comes.

Time spent each day in quiet meditation can give us glimpses of God's timelessness. We see that our schedule is not that important after all, when measured against eternity. As the presence of God seeps into our consciousness, we relax into the fullness and peace of each moment. Trusting our Higher Power to order our lives, we can slow down and enjoy His gifts.

May I exchange hurry and busyness for Your peace.

Communicating

If we do not tell people what is troubling us, they cannot help. We have sometimes been too proud or too shy to let others know what we were feeling. Rather than trying to communicate with those close to us, we ate. Eating instead of communicating further increased our isolation and unhappiness.

Exposing our feelings makes us vulnerable, and we often fear that we will be hurt or rejected. We may be trying to preserve a false image of ourselves as self-sufficient and free of problems. Whatever the reasons for our unwillingness to communicate, we are cheating ourselves. By "clamming up," we cut ourselves off from the care and support of those who love us.

Honest sharing between individuals opens the way for growth and change. By expressing our thoughts and feelings out loud to another person, we become better able to understand and deal with whatever is bothering us. More important, we deepen our relationships with family and friends when we are willing to communicate on a meaningful level.

Give me courage to communicate.

Anger

When angry, many of us overate. Now that we are abstaining, what do we do with our anger?

First of all, we need to be in touch with our feelings so that we can recognize anger when it occurs. In our overeating days, we often may not have realized that we were angry instead of hungry. Not until we were stuffed with food did the anger surface, and then we frequently directed it at ourselves for overeating.

Getting the carbohydrates out of our system allows us to be more aware of our true feelings and reactions. If we can catch our anger when it begins, it is easier to handle. Expressing it in the early stages is less devastating to ourselves and others than waiting until it builds up into a rage.

The best thing we can do with anger is to turn it over to our Higher Power. If we hang on to it, we can be destroyed. Practicing the Steps every day helps us get rid of anger. If we let Him, our Higher Power will take it away.

Take away my anger, Lord.

False Pride

Our pride often gets in the way of our recovery. Not the good kind of pride, the self-respect which belongs to all of us as God's children, but the false pride is what trips us up.

We are falsely proud when we think we can "go it alone," when we recognize no authority higher than our own ego. We are falsely proud when we refuse to ask for help or follow directions. False pride is involved whenever we consider ourselves better than someone else.

As soon as we start off on an ego trip, we are headed for trouble. Sometimes it takes many hard falls before we can give up false pride. Compulsive overeating guarantees that we will learn humility once we recognize that we are powerless over food and cannot manage our own lives.

When we conscientiously examine our motives for overeating and when we look honestly at the damage our wrong thinking has done to ourselves and those around us, we are on the way to getting rid of our false pride. It is something we have to fight continually, since this kind of pride has a way of springing up again and again.

Please forgive my false pride.

Self-Pity

"Poor little 'ole me." The PLOMS. How often do we succumb to this temptation? Usually it's an excuse for not doing what we know we should do, but do not want to do. Or it's a way to manipulate someone else into doing something for us which we should be doing ourselves. If we spend our time moaning and groaning about how unfairly life is treating us, we do not have much chance of discovering the plan which our Higher Power has for us, nor are we able to carry out His will.

Trite as it may sound, the cure for self-pity is to think about those who are less fortunate and to start counting our blessings. Taking some action, doing some small thing for someone else, perhaps a phone call—these are constructive steps to take us off the "pity pot."

When we begin to feel sorry for ourselves because we must follow a food plan and may not eat spontaneously, let's remember where we came from and what things were like before we found OA.

I don't need self-pity.

Habits

Habit can work for us or against us. We have given up a set of eating habits which were counter-productive, and we are learning new ones which will work to our benefit. Some of us require more time than others to make the shift.

Each time we act according to the old, destructive pattern, we re-activate those negative habits. We need to abandon them completely so that they will atrophy from disuse.

Each time we practice a constructive eating habit, we reinforce our new pattern. Writing out a food plan, weighing and measuring the food, eating slowly, and saying no thank you to seconds and binge foods are a few parts of the new pattern. When these actions become habitual, we do not have to think consciously about them, since we perform them automatically. Our mental efforts may then be devoted to something else.

Appetite is largely a function of habit. The more wrong foods we eat, the more wrong foods we want to eat. The longer we follow a healthy, sensible plan, the more it satisfies us.

Teach me to build constructive habits.

Body Signals

When we were overeating compulsively, our bodies seemed to signal constant craving. Now that we are practicing a sane way of eating, we find that our bodies are more responsive to what we put into them.

We discover that we are more satisfied with small amounts of high quality food than we were with vast quantities of junk. Our bodies function better and we begin to hunger for wholesome, natural food rather than the refined sugars and starches we formerly craved.

Before, we never had enough. Now, we eat slowly and give our bodies time to signal cessation of hunger. We finish a meal feeling replete and energized, rather than overstuffed and sluggish. We wake up refreshed after fewer hours of sleep.

Now we can accept periods of hunger before meals as good, rather than something to be feared and avoided at all costs. There is no law against being hungry at times—it adds to the enjoyment of our meals. As our bodies become healthier, we experience them with greater awareness and pleasure.

Make me responsive to the signals of my body.

People Pleasing

If we are too intent on pleasing others, we may lose ourselves. All of us want and need approval from other people, but sometimes we work too hard for external admiration and not hard enough for our own self-regard. If we spend all of our time and energy trying to please others, we never find out who we are and what pleases us.

When we were overeating and felt guilty about that, we may have thought that we needed to do what others wanted us to do in order to somehow make up for overeating. If we didn't look attractive, we could at least be pleasing in other ways!

People pleasing, however, is not confined to those who are overweight. Many people try to find their self-worth and reason for existence in the impression they think they are making on the outside world. It is an easy trap for all of us to fall into.

When we find our center in the life of the Spirit, we become less concerned about pleasing others. As we grow emotionally and spiritually, we begin to discover our giant Self. Through this program, we can find out who we are and what is pleasing to the best that is in us.

May I first seek to please You.

No Doormats Here

When we work the Twelve Steps, we grow in self-respect. Abstaining from compulsive overeating gives us new self-confidence. We no longer need to feel either inferior or superior, but we can take our proper place as an equal to those around us.

Many of us used to let ourselves be manipulated because of a lack of self-respect. We may also have tried to manipulate others. Once we have taken an inventory and gotten rid of past guilts and defects, we embark on a new way of living. Just as we do not try to control the behavior of those we live with, we also do not permit them to control ours.

We are responsible to our Higher Power and responsible for our own actions. We look for opportunities to serve and to give freely of what we have been given. We respect the new life that God has chosen to give us, and we intend to use it as He directs. Saying no to requests and demands which interfere with and jeopardize our program is sometimes necessary for our recovery.

Thank You, Lord, for self-respect.

Abstinence Plus

Most of us find it impossible to maintain our abstinence and our weight loss if we do not continue to grow spiritually and emotionally. The Steps are not something we take once and for all and then put aside. We continue to work on ourselves.

It is possible to reach and maintain a weight goal, but the emotional and spiritual goals of the program are never fully attained. We keep striving for progress, in spite of temporary set-backs.

All of us need something to live for, something that captures our imagination and beckons us on to greater efforts. Achievement in the areas of study and work, commitments to family and community, development of talents and interests—all serve as motivation. Usually, though, we require something more to keep us going. When we become aware of the Spirit which is constantly available to us through contact with our Higher Power, we are tuned in to the source of our abstinence and of our life.

May I remember to live by the Spirit.

Just For Today

I do not have to plan the rest of my life this morning. All I have is today. I do not need to worry about what I will have for dinner tomorrow night. All I need to be concerned about today is today's food plan.

By accepting the fact that I cannot eat spontaneously—whatever and whenever I feel like it—I have freed myself to live more spontaneously. I make plans for the things that need to be done, but I find time left over to use as the Spirit moves. I will not decide today what I will do with that free time tomorrow. Tomorrow will bring new possibilities and promptings.

Just for today, I am living my program. I will not worry about how hard it will be to work it tomorrow. Tomorrow I will have new strength and fresh insight. Just for today, I will remember to stop and listen to the inner voice and follow where it leads. When I follow it, there is adventure in the day and joy in my heart.

Thank You for today.

Rebellion

Compulsive overeating may often be a form of rebellion. In the past, the more we tried to diet, the more we rebelled against the diet, and the more we overate. We were rebelling not only against a diet but also against other people, ourselves, and our Higher Power.

We should never consider abstinence as defined by OA to be just another diet. To do so would be to invite further rebellion. We compulsive overeaters seem especially prone to fight constraints of any kind. Rather than constraining us, abstinence is our liberation. We no longer have a diet to rebel against.

When we accept abstinence, we decide to have three measured meals a day with nothing in between, and we decide to avoid our personal binge foods. What those meals will consist of is our choice, and we make the choice daily. All we have to do is plan what we will have, measure it, enjoy it, and then get from one meal to the next without taking the first compulsive bite. Simple. There is no diet to rebel against.

I pray that I will no longer need to rebel.

Hunger Is a Habit

Have you ever had the experience of being so interested in what you were doing that meal time came and went before you realized that it was time to eat? Because you were not thinking about food, you were not aware of being hungry.

Eating provides a diversion from the tasks of the day. It is something to do when we can't think of anything else to do. Often our "hunger" in anticipation of a meal arises because we look at the clock and see that it is almost time to eat. Instead of being aware of how we are feeling internally, we allow habit and external cues to stimulate our appetite. "It is noon; therefore, I must be hungry."

The more we can concentrate on activities other than eating, the more successful we will be in controlling our disease. We need a program, one which gives meaning to our days and satisfaction to our spirits. Our Higher Power will lift us out of the rut of destructive habits if we sincerely give our lives into His care.

Teach me constructive habits, I pray.

Safety

I am safe as long as I do not take the first compulsive bite. Abstinence is my security. If I break my abstinence, I lose my protection against the confusion, remorse, and pain of overeating.

To keep my abstinence strong, I need to use the OA tools of recovery each day. I need to build my program and to give it my best efforts. Remembering that my Higher Power has given me a new life, I will not endanger it by forgetting how much I need His care.

Temptation is always appearing in one form or another. Sometimes it may seem impossible not to give in. My strength lies not in myself but in God, and only by maintaining close contact with Him can I remain safe.

My Higher Power has led me to OA and has given me a safe place to be. When I am tempted or upset, I will use the telephone, go to a meeting, practice Step Eleven, and do whatever else it takes to maintain my abstinence.

Thank You for bringing me to a safe place.

Resentments

When we hang on to resentments, we poison ourselves. As compulsive overeaters, we cannot afford resentment, since it exacerbates our disease. If we do not get rid of our anger and bitterness, we will suffer more than anyone. Seeking revenge will harm ourselves in the long run.

Many of us have carried around old grudges which caused us to reach for food when we thought about them. We don't need the food and we don't need the grudges, either. When we give away the resentments, we are that much lighter in body and in spirit. Now that we have found OA, we have a way to get rid of the animosity and indignation which has been poisoning our system.

Taking inventory and making amends is an essential part of burying resentments. We need to first be consciously aware of them before we can give them away. These steps usually need to be taken again and again as negative material threatens our physical, emotional, and spiritual well-being.

Take away my resentments, Lord.

Goals

In the OA program, our ultimate goal is not to be able to follow perfectly some diet or other. It is not even to arrive at a certain number of pounds by a certain date. Our goal is nothing short of becoming a new person, the person God intends us to be. Now that is a goal worthy of a lifetime's work!

We begin with the desire to stop eating compulsively. For a while, that may be goal enough. Sooner or later, we discover that in order to stop eating compulsively we need to rely on a Power greater than ourselves, and in the process of developing a relationship with this Higher Power, our goals change.

As our spiritual awareness increases, new possibilities are opened to us. As we experience God's grace in our daily lives, we become less self-centered and more centered in Him. Little by little, our willfulness is absorbed by His will and we are more sensitive to His direction. Our mood changes from one of despair to one of hope, and we grow in willingness to follow wherever our Higher Power leads.

Lord, direct my goals.

A Reason To Be Thin

How many times have we been determined to lose weight for a specific occasion or event? A trip, a wedding, a new job, a holiday—there are many such occasions which may have provided inspiration for short-term reducing. The problem with losing weight for a specific event is that when it is over there is nothing left to provide an incentive for maintaining the weight loss.

Many of us have spent years losing and gaining the same pounds over and over again. Since the reasons for losing were superficial, the loss was temporary.

What we need is a permanent reason to be rid of fat. When we abstain from compulsive eating and work the OA program, we not only lose weight but we also live better. We have more enthusiasm, satisfaction, and peace of mind, as well as better looks and health. Our reason to be thin is that it gives us a richer, fuller life not just for one occasion but every day. The benefits are worth the price.

May I want to be thin for the right reasons.

When I Doubt, Don't

If a particular food is not on our plan, we do not eat it. When in doubt, leave it out. If there is a question in our minds about the advisability of eating a certain food, we are most likely better off without it. Whether we are losing weight or maintaining our weight loss, there will be some foods we choose to avoid, since past experience has proven that we cannot handle them in moderation.

The principle of "when in doubt, don't" may extend to other areas of our lives. If we are unsure of a particular course of action, it is best not to go rushing into it. As we learn to listen to the inner voice, we become more responsive to the leading of our Higher Power. Our knowledge of His will for our lives becomes more solid and we develop a firm basis for decision.

When we are willing to wait for direction, it comes. Indecision may be turned over to our Higher Power for His clarification.

Give us prudence, Lord, to follow Your lead.

Thinking Thin

Our mental attitude has much to do with our physical reality. "As a man thinketh in his heart, so he is." If we think in terms of being thin, it is easier to adjust our appetite to the smaller amount of food which we require. In the past, we may have been eating enough for two people. Large numbers of us in OA have lost the equivalent weight of at least one whole person.

By using our imagination to picture ourselves as thin, active, and healthy, we help our bodies adjust to the new image. Our old, fat self may want more to eat, but the thin person we are becoming does not need more. The fat self may grumble at leaving a comfortable chair to go out for a walk or at climbing a flight of stairs instead of taking the elevator. A sharp mental image of a new, thin self helps provide the necessary motivation to get up and go.

God does not intend us to be distorted and encumbered with excess weight. He will help us see the person we are meant to be.

May I become the person You intend.

Self-Sabotage

There are some times when we seem bent on self-destruction. We may be disgruntled about the demands and responsibilities of the day and determined to punish ourselves for our inability to cope easily. Why we subvert our own best interests is often a mystery, but we all know the frustration and despair of not doing what we should do and doing what we should not do.

Often, we engage in self-sabotage when we are being emotional about a situation instead of viewing it rationally. We usually find that we have forgotten or refused to turn the problem over to our Higher Power. Frequently, we have allowed resentments to build up and cloud our perception.

Whether we turn to food and overeat or whether we indulge in other types of negative, destructive behavior and emotions, we are sabotaging ourselves. We are the ones who suffer the most from our destructiveness. No one else can disturb our serenity unless we permit them to do so.

May I remember to turn to You in times of distress.

Delayed Gratification

One of the advantages of maturity is the ability to delay gratification of desires and needs. It is this ability which makes possible the achievement of long-range goals and plans. We compulsive overeaters have permitted childish demands for immediate satisfaction to drive us into addictive habits. We still have some emotional growing up to do.

When we come to the OA program, we accept a reasonable plan for the gratification of our appetite and hunger. We know that we will eat three times a day, and we choose our food. As our appetite adjusts to eating smaller amounts less frequently, we may experience some discomfort. As maturing individuals, we can accept this discomfort in the interest of a healthier, more attractive body and a saner, more peaceful mind. Instead of having to have what we want now, this minute, we are able to wait until the appropriate time.

Working the Steps makes us aware of the emotional growing we need to do in order to have more satisfying relationships with other people. Here, too, we often have to delay immediate satisfaction in order to achieve larger, more important goals.

I pray for emotional and spiritual maturity.

Miracles

OA testifies to the occurrence of miracles in our daily lives. The physical, emotional, and spiritual changes that take place in those who sincerely practice the program are truly miraculous. Our stories witness to the Power that is available to change lives and produce new people.

These miracles, however, usually happen slowly. It took most of us many years to blow our bodies and minds out of shape by eating too much of the wrong kind of food and by thinking too many of the wrong kinds of thoughts. The miracle of recovery does not happen overnight.

To try OA with the idea of shedding a few extra pounds in time for bathing suit season is to miss the mark. It was lack of self-knowledge and spiritual insight that got us out of shape, and only dedicated, long-term work and commitment to the OA principles will produce the miraculous change we all desire.

Miracles do happen, but the ground needs to be carefully prepared and the new growth nurtured daily.

May I be willing to prepare myself for Your miracle.

Overeating Is Immoral

This planet does not have an inexhaustible supply of food. Those of us who consume more than our fair share are depriving others of their basic needs. While we die early because of obesity-related diseases, others die early from malnutrition and starvation.

We may feel helpless to personally effect a more equitable distribution of the world's food resources. And yet, there are things we can do if we have an honest desire to help. Money which we personally save by eating less can be sent to an organization such as CARE or used to sponsor a child in one of the less-developed countries.

Our country's overconsumption of the world's resources is built up out of the greed of each of us individually. We cannot change the world, but we can be responsible for changing our own behavior. In the process, we benefit the most through better health, positive emotions, and mental peace. Moderate consumption is in our own best interest.

Forgive me for the misuse of Your gifts.

Patience

The person who is a compulsive overeater is often someone who wants what he wants right now, if not before. When we take inventory, many of us realize that impatience is one of our most troublesome character defects. We are impatient with other people when they do not see things our way, we are impatient with the slowness of weight loss, and we are impatient when we do not seem to be making emotional and spiritual progress.

Cultivating patience helps us tremendously with our program. We grow in patience when we give God control of our lives and decide to live according to His timetable. If we accept what happens to us as the will of a Higher Power, we are better able to treat even the unpleasant situations as learning experiences. We become more patient with ourselves when we view our failures as opportunities to try again.

Fruitful growth is slow. Only weeds grow quickly. Acknowledging powerlessness builds the patience to persevere with what we can do and the faith to leave the results to God.

Trusting in You, may I learn patience.

Quality, Not Quantity

We tend to be overly impressed with quantity. How much does it cost? How many friends do I have? How much can I include in my food plan? In a materialistic society, more is synonymous with better.

Before we found OA, we were eating more and enjoying it less. In fact, the more we ate, the more unhappy we became. Greater quantity did not bring better health or a better quality of life.

In this program, we are learning to place quality before quantity. We discover that smaller amounts of nourishing, high-quality foods are more satisfying and make us feel better than vast quantities of empty calories. We become more selective about the way we spend our time, choosing the activities and companions that most enrich our lives, rather than trying to do everything and be everything to everybody. We realize more each day that the quality of our spiritual life is what gives us the inner satisfaction which we sought but failed to find in quantities of things.

Show me how to live well.

Be Good To Yourself

Stuffing ourselves with food which our bodies did not need was not being good to ourselves, nor did it solve our problems. Overeating simply added another problem to the ones we already had.

In the past, when we thought about diets, we may have considered them to be the punishment which we had to undergo in order to get rid of the fat we had acquired. Taking that attitude was not being good to ourselves, either. It is one reason why diets invariably fail, since few of us are willing to endure punishment indefinitely.

The OA program is not a diet but a way of life. It is a way which has worked because it is a positive plan, not a negative restriction. We determine what it is that our bodies need to look and function at their best, and we decide to eat that and nothing else. We are good to our bodies. We also consider what our minds, hearts, and spirits need to function at their best, and we decide that the love and care of a Higher Power is crucial. By working the Twelve Steps, we are good to ourselves.

Thank You for the life that You have given me to live.

Friends Are For Helping

Now that we have found our place in a fellowship of sympathetic friends, we no longer need to be lonely. We have friends who understand us, even though we may only know their first names. Since we are all compulsive overeaters, we share similar experiences and feelings.

Reaching out to others in the program helps us to better understand and accept ourselves. The new life OA gives us needs to be shared in order to be kept. Calling newcomers, sharing transportation, keeping in touch with someone who is having trouble—these contacts strengthen our defenses against old habits and prevent us from slipping back into loneliness. The friends we make through OA are related to us by a deep spiritual bond.

When we are in trouble, we should not be too proud to ask for help. We cannot control this disease by ourselves. Our phone call to another member in time of difficulty is not an imposition but another link in the chain of mutual support.

May I be a giver and receiver of help and friendship.

Take An Idea Break

When we are bored or tired, it has been our habit to reach for something to eat or drink. Food has been our number one stimulant.

There are many sources besides the refrigerator to which we may turn for refreshment. We may stimulate our minds instead of our appetites by reading something worthwhile and thought-provoking. We may listen to music or simply take a good look out the nearest window. In addition to intellectual stimulation, there are many sensory feasts besides food which we may have been neglecting.

During our recovery from compulsive overeating, we grow less obsessed with food and more interested in the world around us. When our brains are no longer dulled with refined sugar, we take pleasure in new thoughts and ideas. The next time we find ourselves thinking about something to eat, let's try consuming something pleasant with our eyes, ears, or minds instead of our mouths.

May I enjoy fully all of the senses and abilities which You have given me.

Different Strokes

Though we are all very much alike as compulsive overeaters, we are also individuals with individual differences. We may work the OA program differently and we may define abstinence differently. The only requirement for OA membership is the desire to stop eating compulsively. Each of us takes a separate path to that goal.

Through the program, we grow more tolerant of the people who think and act differently from ourselves. We share what has worked for us, and someone else is free to take it or leave it. Our attention and concern is of value to those we would help, but we cannot prescribe for them.

Some of us follow a doctor's guidelines for our eating plan. Some of us are not always willing to weigh and measure. Some of us eat smaller, more frequent meals instead of three a day. What is a binge food for one person may be perfectly fine for someone else.

We are all learning how to be responsible for ourselves. No one forbids us this or gives us permission for that. Our differences are God-given, and we accept each other in love.

I need to be more tolerant.

A Democratic Disease

There is nothing snobbish about our disease. It attacks individuals of every social and economic group. In OA, we meet the young and the old, male and female, rich and poor. One of the amazing things about an OA meeting is that it brings together in meaningful communication people from very disparate backgrounds. Even the generation gap closes when a common problem is the focus of genuine concern.

Thanks to OA, we experience warm fellowship. Perhaps for the first time, we come together with other people in a situation where game-playing and ego-building are at a minimum.

To be accepted for what we are and as we are is a healing experience. We may take off our masks and let down our defenses since we do not need to try to impress anyone in OA. As children of God, who happen to be compulsive overeaters, we are all equal.

We give thanks for OA.

Avoiding Extremes

The Greek ideal of the golden mean is a concept which we would do well to ponder. Most of us are extremists, as evidenced by our compulsiveness. We are all or nothing people, and our histories are full of times when we "couldn't believe we ate the whole thing."

Before coming to OA, many of us alternated between starving and bingeing. Either we attempted a diet so limited and stringent that it was impossible to follow for very long, or we indulged our appetites by eating everything that did not move.

OA endorses the practice of moderation. Learning it is difficult for most of us and something which we have been unable to do by ourselves. The members who maintain their abstinence and have a strong program serve as guides and sponsors for those of us who are beginners. Old and new, all of us rely every day on our Higher Power to lead us in the way of moderation.

May I avoid extremes and learn moderation.

Good Spirits

Many of us find that we need to avoid alcohol as well as refined sugars and starches if we are to maintain abstinence. The resemblance between compulsive overeating and alcoholism is striking. Frequently, alcoholics are compulsive overeaters and vice versa.

Both alcohol and sugar induce an artificial high which, in order to be maintained, requires increasing quantities of the addictive substance. Both food and drink may be used as escapes from the unpleasant realities of living, and the abuse of both involves similar character defects.

The spirits found in alcohol and sugar let us down. They are no substitute for faith in a Higher Power and the peace and joy which that faith brings. Alcohol distorts our perception of reality and eventually acts as a depressant. God's Spirit in our hearts clarifies our understanding and gives us enthusiasm and deep joy.

I need Your Spirit, Lord.

A New Boss

When we turn our will and our lives over to the care of God as we understand Him, we have a new employer. From now on, we are working first of all for our Higher Power.

Before, we were probably motivated by egotism, the desire for personal power, prestige, and superiority. Since we were number one, we used our appetites to serve ourselves, with the inevitable result that no amount of food, sex, or material wealth was enough. God did not create us to satisfy ourselves; He created us to serve Him.

Recovering a sense of stewardship may take time for those of us who have spent many years trying to gratify our own desires. We need to pause often each day to ask for God's guidance, so that the work we do, the activities we enjoy, and the thoughts we think may all serve Him. Under His direction, our talents and abilities develop and our appetites serve His purpose.

May my thoughts, appetites, and activities serve You.

Perfectionism

Part of the ego reduction necessary to our recovery is the acceptance of the fact that we are not and never will be perfect. Perfectionism gets in the way of recovery because it imposes impossible, unrealistic goals which guarantee failure. If we do not think we have to be perfect, then we can accept our mistakes as learning experiences and be willing to try again.

Deepening acquaintance with our Higher Power is good insurance against perfectionism. We come to believe that He accepts and loves us as we are, and this gives us the courage and humility to accept ourselves.

We are not perfect, but we are growing. In spite of our weaknesses, we can serve others according to God's plan for our lives. Accepting our own limitations makes us more tolerant of the faults and weaknesses of those around us. Together, we progress.

I am thankful that I don't need to be perfect.

Trick or Treat

Our devious minds have a way of enticing us with visions of sugar plum "goodies" which can trick us into forgetting that we are compulsive overeaters. What may once have been a treat is now, for us, poison. The so-called treat can trick us into taking the first compulsive bite, which we know is always our downfall.

We need to change our thinking so that we no longer consider refined sugars and starches and former binge foods to be treats. Eating them has caused us great unhappiness in the past, and we will not be deluded into thinking that another time will be different.

Through the OA program, we are gaining the self-knowledge which arms us against the assaults of temptation. Our enemy is clever. We need the protection of our Higher Power and the strength that comes from working the Twelve Steps.

Protect me, Lord.

Greedy Thinking, Greedy Eating

Contentment comes from being satisfied with what we have. Since "bread" is a symbol for material things, it is easy to use food as a substitute for the money and possessions we may avidly desire. Overeating can be a form of compensation for the enticing worldly wealth which seems so attractive, yet out of our grasp.

When we desire abstinence more than we desire material things, we are able to maintain it. When we allow material cares and concerns to obscure our spiritual goals, then our abstinence is in danger! Each of us is confronted with the choice of striving to satisfy physical cravings or working towards spiritual ideals. We cannot serve two masters.

We may have thought that we could get rid of our greed for food and continue to indulge our greed for other material things. Our Higher Power does not work that way. He demands nothing less than complete allegiance.

May I serve You without reservations.

Procrastination

This is a particularly dangerous habit for compulsive overeaters, since when we put off unpleasant or difficult tasks, we may revert back to our old escape route—eating. The result is that the unpleasant situation is still with us, and we are less able to deal with it. The longer we procrastinate, the larger the difficulty looms. Even small responsibilities left undone weaken our self-respect.

Often we procrastinate because of fear that we are inadequate for the job to be done. Sometimes we are simply rebelling against doing something we do not want to do. If we are taking a daily inventory, we will examine our motives and use the subsequent self-knowledge for constructive action.

Whatever it is that we are putting off, it will rarely become easier to do later. This is especially true if we are procrastinating about our abstinence! The time is now.

Since today is all I have, may I use it wisely.

Our Security Blanket

Turning to food when we are afraid is a tendency shared by many of us. Since being fed reassured us as infants and children, we compulsive overeaters reach for something to eat when we are anxious or apprehensive. When the anxiety does not disappear, we eat more.

The desire for security is basic to all of us. Unfortunately, we often look for it in the wrong places. A fortress of fat is not much protection against the hurts and dangers to which we are all vulnerable as human beings. Overeating does not keep us safe from real or imagined threats.

We need to accept the fact that there is no such thing as absolute security. All of us are mortal and subject to hazards and destruction. Paradoxically, our security consists in relinquishing our lives to the care of our Higher Power. When we feel safely centered in Him, we have the courage to take risks and give up our worn-out security blankets.

I trust You to care for me, Lord.

More Than Bread

Without a Higher Power, we grasp at material things for security and inspiration. Since they do not give us the ultimate satisfaction we seek, we are left in despair. We need more than bread, but we do not know how to go about getting it.

OA leads us back to the spiritual basis of our lives which we may have lost. All we have to do is be willing to believe in a Power greater than ourselves. When we see what has happened to others who have suffered from the same hunger that plagues us and who have found meaning and fulfillment, we let go of some of our doubt and cynicism.

Lack of faith is perhaps our greatest impediment to spiritual progress. We have been thing-oriented for so long that it is difficult to change. We can agree, however, that the food we overate was not enough to satisfy us. That there is a spiritual source of nourishment which will be adequate to our needs is a conviction which grows stronger the longer we work the OA program.

I pray for the spiritual food which satisfies.

Research

In OA meetings, we sometimes hear reports of "research" done by a member who breaks abstinence in order to find out whether he or she is still a compulsive overeater. The experiment invariably proves that once a compulsive overeater, always a compulsive overeater. Among the results are remorse, regained weight, and weakened control.

It has been said that we are like someone who has lost a leg. We do not grow a new one. We can, nevertheless, learn to live with our disability if we are willing to abstain and follow the OA program. Most of us find that we cannot go back to eating binge foods moderately, but we can avoid them. We are like the alcoholic who can lead a normal, satisfying life as long as he stays away from alcohol.

Further research is not necessary. By accepting our need for a disciplined eating plan, we can benefit from the experience of those who have been in the program longer than we.

May I remember that further research is unnecessary.

Positive Addiction

Since we seem to have addictive types of personalities, we can make this characteristic work for us, rather than against us. We can develop life-enhancing habits—positive addictions.

The OA program is an example of positive addiction. We become habituated to writing down a food plan, attending meetings, making phone calls, working the program. We replace the negative addiction to compulsive overeating with a positive commitment to abstinence.

Other activities which we perform regularly take on the character of positive habits. Exercise is a healthy routine. Hobbies and creative self-expression can be habitual parts of our daily schedule. Whenever we choose a life-enhancing activity and perform it regularly until it becomes an ingrained habit, we are using our addictive tendency to build ourselves up rather than tear ourselves down.

Thank You, Lord, for positive addictions.

Our Barometer

When we find ourselves preoccupied with thoughts of food, we know that something is wrong. Our obsession acts as a barometer which measures emotional pressure. If we are out of tune with our Higher Power, if doubt, resentment, and egotism are taking over, then our disease symptoms begin to surface. It is time to stop and take inventory.

The experiences which other compulsive overeaters share with us give insight into our own behavior. We gain a sharper awareness of our own defects and are less prone to blame external circumstances for our hurts and difficulties.

If we are becoming obsessed with food again, or if we are rationalizing deviations from our eating plan, we need to carefully examine our emotional and spiritual life. Something is out of gear. Concentration on Steps Ten and Eleven is especially important when compulsive thoughts and behavior indicate that all is not well.

Make me sensitive to the state of my emotional and spiritual health, I pray.

Satisfaction Comes From Inside

Why do we continually expect to be satisfied by taking in and possessing things from the outside? Amassing material goods and possessions more often than not stimulates rather than satisfies our appetite. What we do and contribute satisfies us more than what we have and consume.

When we are at peace within ourselves and in contact with our Higher Power, we make fewer demands on the outside world. When we are able to use our abilities in productive work and can give of our emotional and spiritual strength to other people, we feel replete.

Nothing from the outside can bring us happiness if we are at war with ourselves. Chronic dissatisfaction indicates that we have not turned our will and our lives over to God's care, but are still trying to run the show egotistically. Complete surrender opens the way to satisfaction.

I want to surrender to the inner needs of my spirit.

Conflicts

To be alive is to have conflicts. We find our-selves in disagreement with other people and in conflict with ourselves. Often, the things we want seem mutually exclusive, e.g. more money and more free time, more food and fewer pounds.

Our Higher Power does not promise us free-dom from conflict, at any rate, not in this life. Like all growing organisms, we struggle with opposing forces. Frequently, our overeating is an attempt to escape the conflicts which we should be facing. Sometimes we need to be more self-assertive with those around us instead of futilely trying to suppress justifiable indignation with food. There are times when we need to fight for our legitimate requirements.

We cannot always resolve our internal conflicts without a long and difficult battle. Time and maturity are often necessary before a problem is seen in its proper perspective. Some problems we may expect to wrestle with as long as we live. Having faith in the light, even when we cannot see it, makes our darkness bearable.

Lighten our darkness, Lord.

Homesickness

There are certain foods which we will always associate with home and which make us nostalgic to recapture the past. No matter how much we eat, we cannot go back home and be again the babies and little children we were. No food will satisfy our longing for the love, care, and safety most of us associate with home. Even (and especially) if our dependency needs were not met when we were young, eating unnecessary food now will not help.

As we grow in relationship with our Higher Power, we begin to believe that home lies ahead, rather than behind us. We begin to see that our homesickness is for a spiritual state instead of a physical place. Wherever we are, we are pilgrims and travelers, not sure of our final destination but drawn toward something more than what we know in this world. We sense that though we are in the world, we are not of it, that we are homesick for a spiritual fulfillment.

May our homesickness bring us closer to You.

June 19

Taking Inventory

Blaming circumstances and other people for our difficulties, including compulsive overeating, is counter-productive. We cannot control external circumstances or other people, but we can work on changing ourselves. In order to change, we first need to be aware of the attitudes and characteristics which get us into trouble. If we overeat or have a tantrum when we do not get our own way, then we need to learn how to function without demanding that everything should go according to our personal schedule and preference.

We take inventory in Step Four and we continue to take it in Step Ten. It is a valuable tool for our growth. The amazing result is that as we recognize and begin to correct personal defects, our relationships with others improve tremendously. With a positive change in our attitude and behavior, there is a corresponding change in the way other people respond to us.

Taking inventory involves recognizing our good qualities as well as our weaknesses. In OA, we measure our wealth not by what we have but by what we have given.

Teach me to give.

Head Hunger

Those of us who overeat are responding to distorted signals. When we consume food that harms rather than helps our bodies, we are eating in response to some irrational demand in our head rather than because of legitimate physical hunger. The mental obsession with food is an illusion, but one to which we cling with great tenacity.

When we feel "hungry," we need to stop and evaluate the signal. Is it coming from our stomach or from our head? Often, it is after a meal that we most strongly crave something more to eat. This is either because we ate so fast that our stomach has not had time to register satisfaction or because eating has awakened a giant, insatiable appetite for more. It is frequently our mind that wants more, even after our body has had quite enough.

Emotions such as fear, anger, and anxiety can trigger "head hunger." We need perception and insight to know whether the hunger comes from our body or our mind.

May I learn to respond to the legitimate needs of my body.

Discipline

If we think of discipline in terms of punishment, we miss the more constructive meanings of the word. Discipline is order, training, practice, study. Without it, our lives are ineffective and full of chaos. Before we came to OA, our eating patterns were probably chaotic. We may have been short of order in other areas, too.

Discipline is a tool which produces self-respect and a feeling of accomplishment and satisfaction. When we discipline ourselves to eat three measured meals a day, we achieve physical and emotional results which make our spirits sing! The discipline of the OA program liberates us from the tyranny of self-will and self-indulgence.

As we develop trust in our Higher Power, we begin to see that the hardships and difficulties we face are means to spiritual development. Through them, we acquire self-discipline and strength. Our lives become ordered according to God's plan.

Make me willing, Lord, to accept the discipline of an ordered life.

God Is a Verb

We cannot contain our Higher Power at a fixed point or in a closed system. However we may understand God, our understanding is always limited. The Power that rescues us from compulsive overeating is an active force which constantly beckons us to move on. What we were to do yesterday is past; a new day brings new challenges and opportunities.

Our compulsion had us trapped in a pattern of self-destructive repetition. We did the same dumb thing over and over again. When we turn our will and our lives over to the care of God as we understand Him, we are linking up with the source of newness and creativity. God moves, and if we are linked with Him, we also move. His spirit changes us, and what we thought and did yesterday is not adequate to the demands of today.

Trusting our Higher Power means acting according to His promptings. We follow Him as He leads us into new tasks and activities and ideas. We learn from experience that He is always more than adequate for our needs.

May I follow where You lead.

The Everlasting Arms

God moves, and yet He is always here. "Underneath are the everlasting arms." Our former support systems failed us or proved inadequate. We overate because we had no firm ground of support to rely on.

Now we see that since our lives belong to a Higher Power, there is nothing temporal which can remove us from His care and protection. Whatever happens, the everlasting arms are there to uphold us. Knowing that, we no longer need to overeat. We are able to endure whatever comes, whether it is physical hunger, emotional anguish, or spiritual depression.

To experience God's support, all we need to do is admit that we are powerless to sustain ourselves by our own efforts. What a relief not to have to depend on our own ego! If, when we are perplexed and upset, we will stop struggling and take time to be quiet, we will feel the inner peace and support which comes from our Higher Power. The everlasting arms are always here, underneath us.

I need You, Lord.

A Program for Living

The OA program does much more than promote our recovery from compulsive overeating, essential as that is. It gives us a structure for our daily lives. Before OA, we chased illusions and despaired when they let us down. Now we have a concrete plan of action for living richer, fuller lives.

We have found like-minded friends who help and encourage us. Instead of isolating ourselves and consuming, we are experiencing the fellowship of sharing. We find that the more we contribute to OA, the more we get out of it.

Practicing the Twelve Steps involves every aspect of our lives. We cannot be honest in our efforts to work this program without being honest in all our affairs. What we learn about ourselves through OA can be applied to our other activities as well. We were eating compulsively because we did not know how to cope with the rest of life. As we become better equipped for living through the guidance of our Higher Power, we recover from our disease.

Bless our program, we pray.

Abstaining Now

I am abstaining now. I may or may not have abstained yesterday. I make no promises about tomorrow, or next week, or next year, but I am abstaining now.

The most important aspect of abstinence is the quality of life we have when we are abstaining. The quantity of time we have spent being abstinent is secondary. Past days are gone, whether they were abstinent days or overeating days. Now, this present moment, I celebrate the privilege of abstaining.

I will not worry about how long I will be able to maintain my abstinence. All I need to deal with is now. I know only too well what now would be like if I were overeating. I give thanks for the sanity, strength, and peace that my Higher Power gives me when I am abstaining. I give thanks that I may continue safely in the limits of now and let my Higher Power take care of the past and the future.

I thank You that I am abstaining now.

Abstaining Is Not Easy

Abstaining is not easy, but it is much easier than overeating! The reason that we think it easy to overeat is because overeating was a habit. In actuality, processing the extra food was hard on us physically, emotionally, and spiritually.

When we abstain, we break an old habit and learn a new one. The transition requires concentration and dedication. We abstain every minute of the day and night. Even when we are eating, we are abstaining, because we are eating only planned, moderate meals. We are not overeating compulsively, according to whim and irrational pressure.

Some of us apparently have to go through a certain amount of "white-knuckled abstinence" before we arrive at the point where abstaining is easier than not abstaining. Others of us are able from the beginning to relax and abstain comfortably. Whatever our individual experience, we each have available to us the Higher Power that sees us through.

May I stay with You when the way is hard.

You Can Do It

If you really want what OA has to offer, there is nothing that can stop you from succeeding with the program. The program works if we work it. OA does not pass out recovery on a platter, but the tools for recovery are available and proven effective if we are willing to use them.

Go to a meeting today. Re-read your literature. Call another member. Call several members. Get a sponsor, if you do not already have one. Write out what is troubling you. Find a way to be of service to someone else. Abstain now.

Most important, take time to listen to your Higher Power. Ask for the spiritual insight which you need. Remember that you are now committed to following God's will for your life, not your own way. Seek the inspiration that comes from the people and the books which lift up your spirit and show you the way. Then follow.

Lead me, Lord.

Spiritual Awakening

Many of us remember back to a vague time in childhood when our world seemed right and we were full of enthusiasm. Somehow, somewhere along the way, we lost that feeling of rightness and security.

For some of us who experience a spiritual awakening through the OA program, childhood faith is rediscovered and takes on new meaning. We may have lost sight of our real selves and abandoned our original faith in a Higher Power. When we have a spiritual awakening as a result of the Twelve Steps, everything falls into place, and what was lost is recovered, plus much more.

This spiritual awakening continues as we continue to work the program. It gives new meaning to our present lives and new hope for the future. We see that spiritual growth is "where it's at" and that nothing else will satisfy our needs and our longing.

May I continue to awaken.

The Joy of Abstaining

For someone who has suffered the physical, emotional, and spiritual anguish of compulsive overeating, abstaining is not a restriction but a release. We are released from indigestion, lethargy, fat, and the torment of never-satisfied craving.

If we dwell on the negative aspects of abstaining, e.g. the foods we are not eating, we will be unhappy. If we continue to concentrate on food, rather than on life and the spirit, we will find it difficult to abstain. The OA program gives us a new set of priorities and opens the door to new life if we are willing to leave our preoccupation with food outside and walk in.

It is good to feel full of energy rather than full of food. It is satisfying to discover new ways to give. There is deep joy in day by day spiritual growth. All of these joys become ours through abstaining.

We give thanks for the joy of abstaining.

Praise God!

We did not create this program on our own, and we did not achieve abstinence by ourselves. Our recovery is a gift, just as life is a gift. Light, the natural world, our nourishment, talents, love and fellowship—all come from our Higher Power. Our role is to receive, use wisely, share, and enjoy the blessings God has showered upon us.

When we get over the idea that we can do everything by ourselves, we become receptive to the moving force that creates and sustains us. As we stop looking at life from our own egotistical point of view, we begin to see God's glory. No longer a slave to our appetites and desires for material things, we are able to rejoice in our Higher Power and to share our joy with those around us.

Our recovery from compulsive overeating makes us examples of God's power to heal and renew. For all of His miracles, we praise Him.

In You, there is great joy.

Saying No

There are times when all of us find it difficult to say "no." Even though we realize intellectually that we cannot have and do everything, we have trouble saying "no" to the foods, activities, and people that are not good for us.

Abstaining means saying "no, thank you" when offered something not on our food plan. We may think that we are afraid of hurting someone else's feelings by our refusal, but usually it is our own compulsive desire that prevents us from giving a firm no. Our sanity and health are more important than pleasing whoever is offering what we should not have.

As we work the program, we become more aware of the people and activities that use up our energies unnecessarily. Avoiding them gives us more time and strength for what means most to us. Learning when and how to say "no" is a very important part of our recovery. Most often, the person we need to say "no" to is ourself.

I pray for the strength to say "no" to what is not good for me.

Spiritual Strength

What we compulsive overeaters need in order to control our disease is spiritual strength. If we are strong spiritually, we will not turn to food to fill our inner emptiness. We overate because we were spiritually impoverished, and overeating further depleted our spirits.

Paradoxically, we are strongest spiritually when we are most aware of our weakness. In order for our Higher Power to take over, we must recognize and admit our powerlessness. Spiritual strength comes to those who have the necessary humility to receive it.

We do not acquire this strength overnight. The more time we spend each day in communion with God, the stronger we become. Cultivating the awareness of His presence as we go about our activities enables us to rely more and more on His strength and less and less on our own.

Strengthen us with spiritual food so that we do not need to overeat.

Rest In God

Fatigue is one of our worst enemies. Sometimes it is our own unnecessary busyness and over-ambition which wears us out, and sometimes the cause of our fatigue seems unavoidable. Depression and weariness go hand in hand.

It was our habit to reach for something to eat when we were tired. We may still crave refined sugar and carbohydrates as a quick boost when our energy lags. Instead of these substances, which we know will let us down, we need to turn to our Higher Power for rest and refreshment.

Even better than waiting until we are fatigued to ask for help is the habit of resting continuously in God. We may then carry on our activities knowing that we are upheld by His power, and we will avoid the exhaustion of trying to accomplish everything by our own efforts.

May I remember to rest in You.

Holidays

Holidays come and holidays go. Our choice remains the same: to abstain or to overeat.

Most holidays are associated with an over-abundance of special food. Those who are not compulsive overeaters may be able to indulge for a day. We cannot. For us, one day's indulgence is usually the start of a downward skid into loss of control and the despair which follows. What kind of a celebration is it if we end up back in the trap of compulsive overeating?

Every day we may celebrate our freedom by abstaining. When holidays come, we enjoy them more by abstaining than we ever did by indulging. We are free from guilt and remorse and the terrible panic that seizes us when we lose control. We are free to think about the deeper significance of the holiday—whatever the celebration, it is more than a reason to eat and drink.

When abstinence remains the most important part of our life, no matter what day it is, then every day is a celebration and holidays are blessings instead of disasters.

Lord, may I celebrate this day and every day by abstaining.

Ignore the Craving

Old habits die hard, and for a long time we may experience our old craving for that "small," compulsive bite. The craving will not hurt us, and eventually it will pass if we ignore it. If we give in to the craving, it does not go away but becomes stronger. To feed the craving is to pour gasoline on a fire.

When we experience the craving for unnecessary food, we need to find something else to occupy our attention. If possible, we should physically remove ourselves from the tempting situation. If that is impossible, we need to ask our Higher Power for the strength to remain abstinent and to ignore the demands of our over-blown appetite. God never allows us to be tempted beyond our ability to endure. He is always here to support us when we turn and ask for help.

May I listen to You and ignore harmful cravings.

Dual Personalities

It is as if we are each two people. When we are abstaining, we are calm, confident, and capable of handling the demands of every day. When we are in contact with our Higher Power, we have the right mental perspective and God's peace and love in our hearts.

Slipping back into the old attitudes and habits of our compulsive overeating days brings back our frightened, confused, and despairing selves. We lose our ability to function efficiently. We are antagonistic to those around us. Worst of all, we are cut off from the source of strength and light.

Remembering that the negative personality will destroy us makes us more determined not to give in to it. Abstinence, day by day, is our safety. Reliance on the OA group, our Twelve-Step program, and our Higher Power keeps us living the good, new life of freedom.

Deliver me from my negative personality.

Life Is Opportunity

Each morning when we wake up, we thank our Higher Power for another day of abstaining. Each hour that is given to us is a chance to grow and learn and serve. We can believe that God has a plan for every day that he gives us and that He will reveal the plan step by step as we listen for His guidance.

If we are too intent on carrying out our personal ideas and projects, we may miss the directions that come from God. We need to remain open and flexible so that He may use us as He chooses.

Considering the time and tasks that we have as opportunities to serve saves us from self-centered worry and anxiety. We do not have to be compulsive about our work and activities. God knows our capabilities and will not give us more than we can handle. He is always ready to direct our efforts when we turn to Him.

Thank You for the opportunity to live and serve today.

Stronger or Weaker?

Every time I say "no" to the craving for just one small, extra bite, I become stronger. Every time I give in, I weaken myself and make it harder to say "no" the next time.

Abstinence from compulsive overeating is made up of many small decisions. We gradually acquire the knowledge of what we can handle and what we should avoid. This knowledge applies to situations and attitudes as well as food. As we work our program and make the right decisions, we gain strength.

Since none of us is perfect, we do not need to become discouraged when we make mistakes. We are learning how to live, and our failures teach us more than our successes. Growth is slow, but if we keep coming back to OA and the program, we will see results beyond our wildest expectations. OA gives us the strength to become new people.

For growing stronger, we thank You.

Tension or Hunger?

How often have we eaten because of tension, rather than hunger? Accepting our need for three measured meals a day with nothing in between establishes a sensible pattern which satisfies our need for nourishment. When we are tense, we can find ways of relaxing which do not harm our body by making it fat.

Learning to relax the stomach muscles helps get rid of tension-hunger. Often when we have eaten too fast, because of tension, our stomach continues to send hunger signals after the meal. There has not been enough time for the digestive process to register satisfaction. We can consciously relax the muscles so that the feeling of emptiness will go away.

The best cure for tension is a growing faith in our Higher Power. If we are willing to trust Him in the little things of each day, as well as the big events of our life, we will be able to relax and cultivate serenity.

Dissolve my tension and feed my hunger, I pray.

A Progressive Illness

It is the experience of recovering compulsive overeaters that the illness is progressive. The disease does not get better; it gets worse. Even while we abstain, the illness progresses. If we were to break our abstinence, we would find that we had even less control over our eating than before.

Continued abstinence is our only means of health and sanity. We well remember the misery and despair that we felt when we were overeating, and we do not want to feel that way again. Abstaining from one compulsive bite is a small price to pay for health and sanity.

When we find ourselves thinking thoughts which in the past have preceded loss of control, we need to realize the great danger that lies in a relapse. The OA program has saved us from the destruction of compulsive overeating, but our disease is still alive. Our program needs to be foremost in our minds every day if we are to continue recovering.

Do not let me forget my illness.

Goals and Ends

Most of us came into this program with a specific weight goal in mind. We thought that if only we could weigh an ideal number of pounds, all of our other troubles would miraculously vanish.

When we reach goal weight, we discover that we still have to live with ourselves and deal with our problems. If we have been developing a strong program as we have been losing weight, we have a basis on which to work for further emotional and spiritual growth.

Our emotional and spiritual goals are not static. Since we never achieve perfection, there is always opportunity for further progress. The beauty of the OA program is that it is a program for life; its possibilities are limitless. To know and do the will of our Higher Power is our ultimate goal as well as our immediate one.

May I remember that You are my goal today and always.

Growing Up

There is no magic. Nothing—be it person, place, or thing—is going to give us instant and permanent gratification. We keep thinking in the back of our mind that there is some way we can manipulate life into granting us all of our desires, even when they contradict each other.

When we seriously and with honest effort work our way through the Twelve Steps, we begin to grow up emotionally and spiritually. Abstinence from compulsive overeating makes this growth possible. It is not easy, but it is definitely worth the effort.

Acceptance and renunciation are necessary if we are to live with satisfaction in the real world. Grandiose illusions are of no help. We come to understand that certain foods, emotions, and attitudes are not for us if we are to maintain our sanity.

There is no magic, but there is a Power greater than ourselves Who is directing our growth.

Grant me the willingness to grow up.

Living From Within

We are often deluded into thinking that we will find our pattern for living from someone else. We look for models to imitate. Although we do learn from others, it is from within that our most sure guidance comes. Since each one of us is unique, there is no other human being who can give us an example to copy exactly.

OA recognizes individual differences and the need we each have to discover our true self. By sharing our experience, strength, and hope, we are able to develop our unique potential as individuals. We are each free to take from and give to the group, according to our own unique needs and abilities.

If we are to receive the strength which our Higher Power wants us to have, we need to listen to the inner voice that tells us what is right for us at any given moment. The most sure guidance comes from within.

May I listen to Your voice.

Energize, Don't Tranquilize

Food is nourishment for our bodies, not a drug. When we overeat, we sap our energy and dull our responses. Too much food makes us lazy and lethargic. We should eat for energy, not oblivion.

If we have been using food as a narcotic to temporarily deaden the pain of living, then we need to learn other ways to cope. Much of our pain is needless, brought on by egocentric fears and demands. If we accept the fact that we cannot change another person's behavior, then we will not hurt ourselves by anger at what that person does.

At the same time, we will learn to remove ourselves from people and situations which cause us unnecessary pain. We do not have to be martyrs! Abstinence gives us the energy to make positive changes.

A certain amount of pain, both physical and emotional, is unavoidable. Often, it accompanies growth. To tranquilize ourselves with food is to impede growth.

May I remember to eat for energy instead of oblivion.

Clean Abstinence

It is easy to become sloppy in our abstinence and in our program. This is where a daily inventory is an invaluable aid. When we catch ourselves cheating just a little on measurements, making excuses to skip meetings, neglecting to follow the promptings of our Higher Power, it is time for housecleaning.

If we have stopped calling in our food plan and are having trouble with abstinence, we may need to get in touch with a food sponsor. Many of us find it hard to admit that we cannot do everything alone! False pride can be our downfall. If we pretend that all is well when it is not, we cut ourselves off from the help of the group.

The time to correct small mistakes is immediately, before they get bigger and make us discouraged. Admitting the mistake to another person clears the way for correction and change.

Thank You for those who help me maintain clean abstinence.

Hard Right or Easy Wrong?

Constantly we are faced with choices, and often we are tempted to follow the way of least resistance. In our dealings with ourselves and others, it is usually easier to say "yes" than "no," but yes is not always the best answer. If we are too permissive, we become lax and ineffective.

The problem with taking the easy way is that it usually ends up being harder in the long run. If we do not control our eating, we will have all of the problems of obesity. If we do not limit our spending, we will eventually lack funds for what we need. If we do not follow moral and ethical principles, our lives become chaotic and we live in constant fear and tension.

Although choosing the hard right is difficult, it is by exercising our ethical muscles that we become strong and gain self-respect.

By Your grace, may I make the right choices.

The Narrow Path

Abstinence is the narrow path that leads out of the swamp of compulsive overeating. If we allow ourselves to deviate from the path, we immediately put ourselves on slippery ground and run the risk of falling into a bog of quicksand.

The longer we maintain firm abstinence, the more sure our steps become as we walk away from the crippling effects of our disease. It is so much easier to stay on the narrow path than to slip off and have to find it again. Without abstinence, we compulsive overeaters are lost.

If abstinence is not the most important thing in our lives, then food becomes our number one priority, and we gradually destroy ourselves.

Guide my steps, I pray, on the narrow path of abstinence.

Don't Jump

When we have achieved a significant period of abstinence from compulsive overeating, it is as though we have slowly climbed many flights of stairs all the way up to the top floor of a skyscraper. Telling ourselves that we will make a small exception and break abstinence just one time is like saying we will jump out a window on the top floor of the skyscraper and fall down only as far as the next floor.

The nature of our disease is such that one small compulsive bite inevitably leads to eventual disaster. We may be able to postpone the binge for a day or a week or even longer, but once we give up our control, we put ourselves in a pattern of downward descent.

All we need do in order to stay on the top floor of the skyscraper is to maintain our abstinence. A small price to pay for such a magnificent view.

Protect me from a fatal jump.

Right Makes Might

When we are working our program properly, we have an inner sense of rightness that makes us strong and self-confident. We are controlling food, rather than being controlled by it. We are willing to let our Higher Power straighten out our confused lives.

Action is necessary. We need to "walk the walk" as well as "talk the talk." No amount of insight will give us progress unless we are willing to take the concrete steps outlined in the OA program. We need to work closely with qualified sponsors who can guide us in our abstinence and in our program.

Compulsive overeating made us weak physically, emotionally, and spiritually. As we abstain, we gain strength on all three levels.

Thank You for the strength that comes from doing the right thing.

Turning Toward the Light

Plants, as they grow, automatically turn toward the light. People can choose between light or darkness. The OA program is available to us, but we may choose whether or not we will follow it. Our Higher Power is also available to us, if we choose to seek His will.

Before we found OA, we wandered around in the darkness of compulsive overeating. Now that we see glimmers of light, we need to turn ourselves in the direction from which the light is coming. Working the program requires taking the time and effort to change our routine. The light is here, but we need to turn away from darkness and open ourselves to it.

As we examine ourselves in the light that comes from our Higher Power through OA, we begin to see more clearly where we should make changes and how we may find health and peace.

Grant us grace to turn toward Your light.

Following the Rules

When we were eating compulsively, we thought we could make up our own rules as we went along. We thought we were entitled to eat what we wanted when we wanted it. The result was chaos. We found that living according to self-will did not work.

Commitment to the OA program involves the willingness to accept a set of rules which we did not make. Following the abstinence guidelines is what enables us to control our disease. When we ignore the discipline which has worked for others and insist on doing it our way, our chances for recovery diminish.

The rules of abstinence—three measured meals a day with nothing in between, no binge foods, a definite plan, etc.—are the means to freedom. To rebel against them is to delay or prevent our liberation from compulsive overeating.

I pray for the honesty to follow the rules.

The Power of Abstaining

Abstaining from compulsive overeating fills us with new strength. When we become honest and determined in this area of our life, our resolution and clarity flow into other areas, too. The new order and discipline is reflected in all that we do.

We establish abstinence as the most important thing in our life. As mind and body are released from the dullness and apathy caused by too much food, we are more efficient and we function more effectively. Other priorities and values sort themselves out. Instead of being torn by conflicting desires, we are able to decide which projects and activities are of most value. Instead of being paralyzed by fear and depression, we have the motivation and energy to do what needs to be done.

Accepting life-long abstinence as the will of our Higher Power enables us to push food out of the center of our life.

Thank You for the power of abstaining.

Food: Servant or Master?

Food used to be our master. The mental obsession with food and the craving for more controlled our life. As we recover, we begin to see just how much we were in slavery to food and our appetite. We know that no matter how long we abstain and recover from our disease, we will always be powerless over food. The idea that we will one day be able to eat spontaneously is the most dangerous delusion we can entertain.

By abstaining from compulsive overeating every day of our life, we make food our servant rather than our master. We eat what we need to nourish our body, but we do not permit eating for comfort, excitement, or any other emotional reason. Whatever it takes to remain abstinent is what we are willing to do each day.

Never forgetting that we are always one mouthful away from a binge insures that food will remain our servant.

Today and every day, may I serve You instead of food.

Living Is a Privilege

When we were overeating, how often did we drag ourselves out of bed wondering how we were going to make it through the day? Many of us felt that life was treating us unfairly, and we blamed those around us for our misery. We may have thought we believed in a Power greater than ourselves, but we were unable to apply the belief so that it made a difference in the way we were living. Trying to manage our own life pushed us farther and farther into despair.

The OA program shows us how to commit our will and our life to the management of God. We stop trying to "go it alone," and we listen for His direction. By the grace of our Higher Power, we abstain from compulsive overeating one day at a time, and we walk a new way of humility and obedience.

Little by little, we recover in mind and body, and we no longer feel crushed by an uncaring fate. We accept each day as a gift from the hand of God, and we live it to the best of our ability.

Thank You for the privilege of living and abstaining today.

Gifts

The OA program is a gift to us from our Higher Power. Without it, we would still be bogged down in compulsive overeating with no solution in sight. Our fellowship gives us the hope and love we need to sort ourselves out and begin to live a new life.

Recovery through abstinence is the gift which we are offered every day. In order to receive it, we need to be sincere and earnest in our efforts to work the program. We can count on God's support if we are willing to go to any lengths to stop eating compulsively.

With gratitude for these gifts from our Higher Power, we are able to give back what has come to us. We share our program and give our time and abilities where we see a need that we can fill. The more we give, the more we receive. God's abundance is inexhaustible.

We thank You for Your gifts.

Doing God's Will

For a long time, most of us tried to achieve happiness by serving our self-will. We figured out what we wanted from life and then went about trying to attain it. When our efforts were frustrated, we turned to food and overeating.

The idea of giving our self-will to God and following His direction makes us fearful. We fear that we will lose out and be unhappy. We are reluctant to give up our illusions of autonomy and power. We wonder if there really is a Higher Power who can direct our way. We pray for guidance and then forget to listen for the response.

When we are willing to trust a Higher Power in even one small area of our lives, we begin to see results. As our faith grows, we become confident enough to relinquish more and more of the concerns which by ourselves we are unable to manage. The more we work this program, the more sure we are that our peace and happiness lie in serving God, rather than ourselves.

I pray for courage to follow Your will.

OA Unity

When we come into OA, we are amazed to find so many other people with the same problems and difficulties. We are even more amazed at the stories we hear of the successful solution of these problems which have defeated us for so long.

We are united in our common illness—compulsive overeating—and we are united in our common program of recovery—abstinence and the Twelve Steps. What we could not accomplish alone, by our own efforts, becomes possible through the strength of the group and the Higher Power.

Each of us is responsible for the life of OA. We each have a role to play and an area in which to serve. If we do not do our part, the organization as a whole is weakened. By our service to the common goals, our own program is strengthened. "Letting someone else do it" will not work. Saying "yes" when there is a job that I can do is what maintains OA unity and my own recovery.

May I contribute to OA unity.

God Cares

It may be hard to believe that the Power of the universe is concerned with everything we do, including how and what we eat. The awareness that God does indeed care about the minute details of our daily existence comes to us as we see evidence of that care. When we turn to Him and trust His support, we see that our lives go more smoothly.

When we are relying on our Higher Power for the little things as well as the big ones, our timing improves. We are at the right place at the right time. We do not waste energy trying to do what we are not meant to do. The way opens up in front of us and we pass through difficulties unscathed.

We can believe that God is concerned with our recovery from compulsive overeating. He is health and wholeness, and we are made in His image. All that prevents us from receiving His healing care is our ignorance and self-will. Through this program we learn how to accept God's care.

We are grateful for the knowledge that You care.

Always Abstinence

As recovering compulsive overeaters, we have a fixed, focal point of reference. Abstinence is the most important thing in our lives without exception.

What began as weakness has become strength. Whatever happens to us, we know that by maintaining abstinence we will be able to cope. As long as abstinence controls our self-destructive, inner enemy, we are able to function effectively.

This does not mean that we will be free from problems. Abstaining does not get rid of all of our difficulties. There will be times when we are depressed, anxious, afraid, angry, bored, and in pain. To be alive is to be subject to these negative emotions, as well as the positive ones which we enjoy.

By abstaining, we are able to face reality instead of escaping into a worse predicament. No matter how difficult the day, it has been a good one for the compulsive overeater who has abstained.

I pray for abstinence always.

Focus on Living

Before we found this program, we were obsessed with food and preoccupied with eating. Instead of concentrating our energies on love and work and play, we were side-tracked into the unsatisfactory substitute of overeating.

Abstinence gives us a new lease on life. We can develop more satisfying relationships with our family and friends. Since it has been our habit to withdraw and please ourselves with food, it takes time and effort to learn to relate more closely to those we love. It also takes courage and the willingness to be open and vulnerable.

In our work, we have renewed energy and greater ability to concentrate. Where before we may have avoided difficult tasks, we now have the strength and confidence to attempt them.

When we give up eating as a favorite form of recreation, we can find other activities to enjoy. Being released from bondage to food and fat opens the door to all sorts of new possibilities. Less eating means much more living.

We are grateful for new life.

Inner Guides

In a crisis situation, we cannot rely on another person, or a book, or any external source to tell us what to do. We may have to act immediately, and there may be no outside help available.

By getting in touch with our Higher Power, we cultivate a never-failing source of inner strength and direction. In order to have it available when we need it, this inner voice must be consulted habitually. It is not something which we may call on in times of emergency and forget about when things are going well.

Each of us has this inner source of strength and nourishment. By taking time each day to withdraw from the distractions of the external world, we grow in spiritual knowledge. When the chips are down, this spiritual strength which we develop by daily prayer and meditation is what will see us through.

May I know You more clearly each day.

Promptings

If we are listening, we will hear promptings from the inner voice. Often they are suggestions for small acts of kindness and love. Sometimes they are urgings to do a difficult deed in order to correct a wrong or to apologize for a mistake. Whatever the prompting, we are free to ignore it or act on it.

Often, ignoring the prompting would appear to be the easiest course. Why should we go out of our way to help someone else, particularly if that person is a stranger? Apologies are frequently embarrassing and deflate our pride. Reaching out to someone with love makes us vulnerable to rejection, and we fear exposure.

In the long run, to ignore the promptings of our inner voice is to commit spiritual suicide. These promptings are intended for our growth, and if we do not grow in love, we will atrophy and decay. Through the Twelve Steps, our Higher Power leads us to do many things which we would prefer to avoid but which insure our recovery.

I pray for willingness to follow the promptings of the inner voice.

Motivation

Most of us fight the temptation to be lazy, to get by with doing the minimum instead of our best. When we were children, we had parents and teachers who urged us on to greater efforts. As adults, we have to depend more on internal motivation and less on the exhortations of others.

Working for strictly material goods is not enough to provide the impetus and enthusiasm we need. It is our Higher Power who gives us our talents and abilities, and it is His plan for their use which we seek to follow.

Doing less than the best we can is short-changing ourselves. We miss the satisfaction that comes from stretching as far as we can. We also miss the opportunity to exceed former limits. The more we do, the more we are able to do.

Motivation comes from our Higher Power and can only be received as we are willing to act. Thinking and planning have their place, but it is action which generates fresh enthusiasm.

May I live up to the maximum of my abilities today.

Speaking From the Heart

Through the OA fellowship, we offer each other mutual support. Since we believe that the Higher Power works through the group, what one of us is prompted to say is probably just what another member needs to hear.

Sometimes we are reluctant to speak of what is in our heart for fear of being embarrassed, belittled, or betrayed. We are so accustomed to masking our true feelings that we often lose touch with them. In OA, we are assured that what we say will be received in a spirit of acceptance and love. We do not need to be afraid of revealing our deeper selves.

It is a healing experience to belong to a group which is dedicated to honest communication with a minimum of game-playing. When we make a genuine attempt to describe where we are in our program, we are met with a warm and supportive response. Our Higher Power opens the way for meaningful communication and mutual love.

Open our hearts to You and to each other.

God's Time

When we feel under pressure and fear that there will not be enough time to do the things we think we need to do, it helps to stop for a moment and remember that all time is God's. We may be wanting to do more than we should in the same way that we wanted to eat more than we needed. Exchanging compulsive overeating for compulsive activity is no solution to our problem.

Turning over our lives to our Higher Power as we begin each day allows Him to schedule what we will do and when we will do it. He knows our capabilities even better than we do, and He does not give us more to do than we can manage. To benefit from His guidance, we need to stay in touch with our inner selves and not get swept away by external demands.

In the past, we may have alternated between periods of non-productive lassitude and frantic bursts of activity. As we maintain ourselves on an even keel physically by abstaining from compulsive overeating, we learn moderation and order as God shows us how to use the time He gives us.

Please order the time which You give me every day.

Future Phobia

Irrational worry about the future may have triggered eating binges before we found the OA program. Learning to live one day at a time is a necessary part of controlling our disease. Our instinct for security must not be allowed to run riot any more than the other instincts we are learning to control.

Trusting our Higher Power today insures that we will trust Him tomorrow also. We do not know what the future holds for us, but we are assured of God's continuing care and support. To entertain irrational worries about what might or might not happen is to doubt the Power which is restoring us to sanity. When we take Step Three without reservations, we give up our crippling anxieties.

We do not expect that life will be a rose garden in the future, any more than it is right now. There are problems and disappointments and pains to deal with. What we do expect is the strength to cope with whatever our Higher Power gives us, realizing that the difficult experiences are often the ones from which we learn the most.

May faith in You blot out fear.

Planting Seeds

The closer we walk with our Higher Power, the more effective our Twelfth Step work is. We always remember that the best thing we can do for other compulsive overeaters is to maintain our own abstinence. Beyond that, we are given opportunities to spread the word as we go about our daily activities.

Mentioning what OA is doing for us may open the door to a new life for one of our friends. It may be a casual acquaintance or even a stranger who needs to hear about the program. Our instincts can guide us as to the best time and place to share news of our recovery.

Often, we may not know what effect, if any, our witness has had on another person. We may be annoyed if we are unable to "sell" the program to someone we think should have it. The results of our Twelfth Step work are in the hands of our Higher Power, and positive effects may show up long after we have planted a seed.

Show me where I may plant seeds of recovery.

Keep It Simple

Complicated food plans and complicated lives work against us in this program. We compulsive overeaters have a hard time making decisions about food, and the more simple our menus, the better. We also tend to overextend ourselves in other areas, dissipating energy which we need for working our program.

Our three meals a day can be nourishing and attractive without being elaborate. If we spend too much time and energy planning and preparing our food, we run the risk of reactivating our obsession. Too much thinking about food usually leads to overeating and invariably produces mental turmoil.

For our peace of mind and emotional serenity, we need to keep the mechanics of our lives as simple as possible. If the spirit is to be free, it cannot be shackled by overconcern with material things.

May I keep life simple today and use my energies for working the program.

Reflecting Light

We are made to reflect the goodness and light of our Higher Power. In order to do this, we need to be as free as possible of the negative emotions and self-will which block out God's light. The light is always here. It is our job to keep ourselves free from the entanglements and hang-ups which cloud our vision.

Our primary means of staying in the light is to abstain from compulsive overeating. Without clean abstinence, we become muddled in our thinking and in our emotions. God's light and love can shine through our lives if we are physically ready to receive and reflect.

Working the Steps frees us from the negative emotions which block out the light. At first we may have wondered how the Twelve Steps were related to our problems. As we progress in the program, we see that without the spiritual growth which they facilitate, we cannot be fully open to the light from our Higher Power.

Prepare me to reflect Your light.

Daily Inventory

When we are not functioning up to par, we need to find out where the problem is. If the day begins to fall apart and we feel overwhelmed and unable to cope, it may be a good idea to stop and take inventory.

Examining the quality of our abstinence is a good place to begin. Have we permitted thoughts of making a small exception here and there? Are we dwelling too much on what we will have for the next meal? Did we make a substitution which gave us more carbohydrates than we could handle?

If the problem is not with abstinence, then it must be in our emotional or spiritual life. Are we harboring resentments which are poisoning our outlook? Have we made a mistake which we are unwilling to admit? Is there something we need to do for a family member that we are procrastinating about doing? Are we denying a legitimate need of our own?

Grant me the honesty to confront my weaknesses.

No Compromises

Where abstinence is concerned, there can be no compromising. In order to control our illness, we are willing to go to any lengths to maintain abstinence. Nothing else is as important to us.

If we are eating in a restaurant where the right kind of vegetable is not available, we can order two salads or do without a vegetable for one meal, rather than substitute a starch which will activate our disease. We learn what we can handle and what is not for us, and then we act on that knowledge in every situation. To compromise "just this once" is an invitation to trouble.

Just as we have a certain way of eating for the maintenance of our recovery, so we have a way of living based on the principle of rigorous honesty. Honesty in all of our activities is what makes us strong and effective. Where the core principles of our program are concerned, we do not compromise.

By Your grace, may I maintain my integrity in all situations.

Sloppy Thinking

If we begin to entertain thoughts of slight deviations from our food plan, thoughts of former binge foods, thoughts that maybe once in a while we could eat "normally," we put ourselves on shaky ground. Our disease is never cured, and sloppy thinking can lead to a weakening or loss of control.

"Normal" eating for us is abstinence. Our food plan is what saves us from bizarre eating behavior. There is no such thing as taking a vacation from abstinence.

The less we think about food, the better off we are. To remember the so-called pleasure we once associated with certain foods may cause us to forget the inevitable pain and anguish which eating them eventually produced. We do not want to ever return to the misery of compulsive overeating.

Giving our minds to our Higher Power insures positive, healthy thinking.

Take my thoughts, Lord, and straighten them out.

The Beacon

There are times when we get tired and depressed or elated and confused. We are mentally uncomfortable, knowing that something is wrong but unable to pin-point the trouble. Our first thought may be to reach for food, but we know that way leads to disaster.

We compulsive overeaters have a beacon light for our dark and confused moments. It is our commitment to abstinence. No matter how confused we may be, we can remember that abstinence is the most important thing in our life without exception. Whatever happens, we will not be lost if we hold fast to our abstinence. From that commitment, everything else follows. As long as we do not overeat, we will be able to find our way out of a difficult situation.

Our Higher Power gives us the beacon light of abstinence, and with it He gives guidance out of our perplexities. Patiently waiting until we clearly see His will keeps us from getting lost in the darkness of self-will.

Thank You for the beacon light of abstinence.

Be Prepared

We need to be prepared for times when we will be tempted to eat the wrong kind of food. This may mean eating our abstinent meal before going to an event where the right food may not be available. It may mean adjusting our meal schedule so that we can wait to eat until after an event where the wrong kind of food is served.

In the past, we may have used the excuse of not hurting someone's feelings in order to rationalize a deviation from our food plan. No hostess should expect a guest to consume food to which he is allergic. We alone are responsible for what goes into our mouths. If we are faced with food which will activate our illness, it is better to be hungry than to eat what makes us sick.

When we are willing to go to any lengths to maintain abstinence, we can find a way to deal with dangerous food situations. "No, thank you" is a very useful tool.

May I be prepared for times of temptation.

Rationalizing

We compulsive overeaters are experts at making excuses for taking the line of least resistance. Before we entered this program, we could always find a reason for eating. How many times did we say, "Just one little bite can't possibly hurt"?

It is hard to say "no" to ourselves and to other people, even though we may realize that saying "yes" would be hurtful to our health or our integrity. We think up reasons for going along with what other people want us to do, rather than "rocking the boat" by standing up for what we know to be essential for our recovery.

Often we convince ourselves by rationalizing that all is well when it is not. Our emotional and spiritual health require that we examine honestly our behavior and our relationships. When they are not right, we need to take action to correct them.

By Your light, may I see clearly.

Inner Tigers

What we fear facing and dealing with is often inside. We may transfer our fear and irritation to external circumstances and the people around us, when what we need to do is look inside. Usually, we are our own worst enemy.

Our fears go back to a time when we were very young and relatively helpless. We may still be afraid of rejection, of being inferior, of being hurt with no one to take care of us. We may have an irrational fear of economic insecurity which comes from a time when we were aware of financial problems but too young to understand them.

Whether our inner tigers are real or made out of paper, we need to face them instead of eating to appease them. As we recover from compulsive overeating, many of the fears which we had tried to bury with food come to consciousness. With the Power greater than ourselves, we are able to tame the inner tigers.

Secure in Your care, may I not fear self-discovery.

Today Is the Day

Many of us have spent most of our lives dreaming of the day when we would be thin and attractive and able to do the things we want to do. We have put off living to some indefinite time in the future. As long as we were fat, we had a reason to avoid challenges and delay satisfactions. By not attempting to realize our dreams, we averted the risks of failure and the possibilities of success.

The OA program teaches us how to live today. One step at a time, we begin today to do the things we were putting off until tomorrow. We learn that we can live now, day by day, instead of waiting for the future.

Abstaining from compulsive overeating brings self-respect and determination to develop our unique potential. The time to get a job, take dancing lessons, be a friend—that time is now, today.

Thank You for the opportunities of today.

Punishing Ourselves

Most of us have been carrying around a load of guilt. We felt guilty about overeating and periodically used dieting as a form of self-punishment. We felt guilty about not being perfect, and we felt guilty unless we said "yes" to everything that everyone expected of us.

In this program, we learn to accept the fact that we are human and not perfect. Through the Steps, we are able to get rid of unnecessary guilt and make a fresh start each day. We do not need to continue to punish ourselves for past mistakes, either by overeating or by denying our legitimate rights as individuals.

Abstinence gives us freedom from compulsive overeating and freedom from self-punishment. We give our bodies what they need, and we also nourish our minds, hearts, and spirits. In our fellowship and in our contact with God as we understand Him, we experience the Power of love which wipes out guilt.

I am glad to learn that self-punishment is no longer necessary.

Self-Respect

When we were overeating, we did not have much self-respect. Because we felt guilty about the quantity of food we were consuming and the way we looked, we had a very poor self-image. Since we did not respect ourselves, we did not act in a way which evoked respect from others. We put ourselves down and allowed other people to use us.

Abstinence and the OA program produce a change which is often astonishing. Our self-respect grows in direct proportion to the control we acquire. When we stop overeating and begin to live in accordance with the will of our Higher Power, we can accept and respect ourselves. Those around us respond to us differently as our own attitude improves.

What we realize is that self-respect and inner acceptance is more important than any external approval or disapproval. Instead of living for the admiration of others, we seek each day to follow the will of our Higher Power.

I am grateful for the self-respect that OA has given me.

Highs and Lows

Abstaining from compulsive overeating does not guarantee that we will always be on an even keel emotionally. We continue to have ups and downs, and often we feel emotional distress even more keenly when we are no longer using food as a narcotic.

Part of our program involves the striving for balance and perspective. Experience teaches us not to get carried away by either elation or depression. These are moods which will not last, and we prefer to base our actions on the rational decisions which we make in times of quiet reflection.

Contact with OA friends during periods when we are either high or low helps to put our emotions in perspective. By expressing what we feel, we are better able to deal with it. Some of us tend to make calls when we are up and others of us reach for help when we are down. Ideally, we will make contact both times so that we may strengthen each other and learn not to be overwhelmed by mood swings.

May I remember that You can control my highs and my lows.

Togetherness

In this program, we are able to do together what none of us could achieve alone. We may have tried many ways to control our disease before we came to OA, but they did not work or we would not be here.

We share a common illness and a common cure. Abstinence is possible as we share it with each other. The program works as we work it together. Each of us is an individual, but we function best with the support of the group. If we neglect to go to meetings and make phone calls, we cut ourselves off from the strength and inspiration we need.

Our Higher Power works through each of us as we share what we have been given. We do not achieve and maintain abstinence by ourselves. Most of us overate alone. Learning to live without overeating involves learning to live with other people. Our fellowship is our recovery, and together we grow.

Thank You for our togetherness.

False Gods

Our Higher Power is that which we turn to in times of stress. In the past, we turned to food, thus making it in fact our Higher Power, even though we may not have realized what we were doing. Food is not capable of being a Higher Power for anyone; food is a thing. By turning to food in stressful situations, we cheated ourselves with a false god.

Lurking in the back of our mind, there may still be some false gods. We may think that more money or an exciting love affair would give us permanent security and happiness. The desire for popularity may be deluding us into thinking that we can please everyone if we try hard enough.

The beauty of the OA program is that it shows us, day by day, the Higher Power who will not let us down. As we see our false gods for what they are, we grow in truth. Daily communion with God as each of us understands Him gives us an intimate relationship with the One to whom we can turn in times of stress.

Thank You for revealing my false gods.

Emotional Abstinence

When our eating was out of control, our emotions were also out of control. Even after we accept physical abstinence from compulsive overeating, we may still go on emotional binges. This indulgence leaves us depleted and hungover and wreaks havoc in our relationships with those we love.

The Twelve Steps are our guide to emotional abstinence. They are the means by which we can live without being destroyed by anger, envy, fear, and all of the other negative emotions. Working the Steps frees us from our slavery to self-centered, irrational reactions which harm ourselves and others.

Realizing the damage which comes from hanging on to anger and resentment, we gradually become able to turn these feelings over to our Higher Power before they get out of hand. Accepting ourselves means that we can accept others for what they are without trying to manipulate them or expect them to be perfect. Controlled by our Higher Power, we learn to avoid emotional binges.

May I remember the importance of emotional abstinence today.

Envy

When my inside looked at your outside, I overate. Envy of what others seemed to be and of the possessions they had was a prime trigger for overeating, turning to food to compensate for an apparent lack. No amount of food can satisfy envy.

Why is it that the other person seems so much more fortunate, or talented, or happier than we? We are painfully aware of our own inadequacies and quick to envy whoever appears to "have it together." Looking at the outside image or mask is deceptive, however, and prevents us from seeing that underneath is a fellow human being beset with problems and difficulties just as we are.

Who we are, where we are, and what we have is God's gift to us. What we do with ourselves is our gift to God. The more we seek to do His will, the less we envy our neighbor's abilities and possessions. The peace of mind we receive through this program fills us with such gratitude that there is increasingly less room for envy.

Take away my envy, I pray.

Exercise

We are made to be physically active. When we were loaded down with food and fat, we probably moved around as little as possible. Now that we eat for health, we have the necessary energy to exercise our bodies.

Taking the stairs rather than the elevator, walking instead of riding, a few simple calisthenics when we need a break from work, a jump rope—there are many ways to begin an exercise program in easy stages. We do not need to train to become Olympic athletes, but we do need to keep our bodies in good working order.

Each day we also need mental, emotional, and spiritual exercise. Reading something worthwhile, refraining from criticism, performing a service for someone anonymously, taking time for prayer and meditation—these are actions which develop our minds, hearts, and spirits. Our growth in the program depends on overcoming resistance and inertia each day and taking concrete steps to improvement.

By Your power, may I overcome laziness.

Being Available

In our search for security, we turned to food in times of stress. Now we are growing in reliance on our Higher Power instead of food. We do not, however, "use" the Higher Power the way we tried to use food. We do not use God; He uses us.

What we do is make ourselves available to the Higher Power, and open to light and guidance. We pray each day that we may do His will, not ours. Often this means a more flexible schedule than we may have had in the past. Since the Higher Power is ever creative and new, we cannot cling to our old routines and habits. To insist on our time, our way, our plan, is to block out God's guidance.

Sometimes we may be called on to perform a service which means giving up our plan for the day. When the prompting comes from deep within, following it will further our growth in the program.

Today I will be available for Your use.

A Living Program

The Twelve Steps are a program for living and they are also a living program. Taking them is not something we do once and for all, but something we repeat over and over in greater depth. They are our guidelines for each day.

Our program develops as our understanding matures. When we first join OA, physical abstinence from compulsive overeating may be all we can handle. As we learn from fellow members and are increasingly exposed to the power of the group, our program comes to include more emotional and spiritual elements. The possibilities for development are limitless.

One thing leads to another. The creative force that guides OA directs our individual efforts. When we are open to the challenges and willing to give up self-will, we make progress which gratifies and astounds us. This program not only works as we work it; it also grows as we grow.

We thank You for Your creative spirit.

Accepting Reality

Failure, death, divorce, disease, betrayal—these are all part of the world we live in. We agonizingly search our minds to figure out why, but are unable to come up with any satisfying answers. We pray for the serenity to accept the reality of life.

Previously, we tried to deny reality by overeating. What that did was make reality worse for us. Abstaining from compulsive overeating and working the steps of the OA program gives us the strength to cope with reality and accept the things we cannot change. We often feel as though we are on a long uphill climb. Let's not forget that if it were not for abstinence and our Higher Power, we would be rapidly sliding downhill.

Whatever our situation, it is better to face it squarely than to delude ourselves with excess food. None of us escapes pain and suffering. By turning them over to our Higher Power, we are strengthened by our hardships, rather than destroyed.

May we have the courage and strength to accept life as it is.

Willingness

When we were overeating, we were negative and fearful. We alternated between avoiding work and feeling responsible for everybody and everything. An important part of our recovery is willingness: we become willing to change, willing to abstain, willing to learn. As we work the program, we become willing to allow our Higher Power to remove our character defects.

All of this does not happen overnight. When we get discouraged and make mistakes, we are willing to try again. We are willing to follow the lead of our Higher Power. As we see evidence of His care, we begin to trust that He will not require of us more than we are capable of doing.

To be willing is to hold ourselves ready and available for God's direction. We do not jump into situations prematurely, and we do not close our minds in refusal to change. We are willing to grow and serve and, especially, willing to believe.

Increase my willingness.

Love God and Work the Program

How clear everything becomes when we put abstaining and recovering from compulsive eating first in our lives! As we recover, we grow in love for the Higher Power which makes possible our new life. Loving God and working the program becomes our main purpose every day. From this, all else follows.

When we are confused and harried by conflicting demands on our time and attention, we need to withdraw for a moment and get back in touch with the God within. As long as we are sincerely trying to do His will, we do not have to be upset by negative responses from other people, whether their disapproval is real or imagined.

As our Higher Power provides a focus for our love, working the program provides a focus for our energies and ambitions. Whatever our situation, we are each capable of growing along spiritual lines, and it is this growth and progress which gives us deep, lasting satisfaction.

Accept my love and work.

Getting Honest With Ourselves

The day that we realize that we are and always will be compulsive overeaters and that we can permit ourselves no deviousness when it comes to food—that is the day when we begin to take the OA program seriously. Half-measures do not work. Lingering exceptions in the back of our minds will defeat us. Beginning the program with the idea of quitting when we have lost a certain number of pounds will not bring success.

Nothing short of an honest, wholehearted commitment to abstinence and the OA program will give us the ability to stop eating compulsively. If we think we can get away with small deviations here and there, we are deluding ourselves. Our disease is progressive, and unless we take the steps outlined in the program, it will eventually destroy us.

If we are not honest with ourselves, we are divided, weak, and sick. Getting honest means getting strong and well.

May I be directed by the truth.

Accepting Guidelines

Some of us have gone through life thinking that we did not need to follow any guidelines. Somehow, we got the idea that special circumstances placed us above the rules. We looked for shortcuts and rebelled against the tedium of discipline. Considering ourselves exceptional, we decided to make our own guidelines. These were usually based on doing what we felt like when we felt like it.

When we get to OA, we may spend a short or a long time experimenting with the program, adjusting it to suit ourselves. Sooner or later, we discover that our adjustments do not work. The OA program works, provided we follow the rules and work it as it is, not as we might like it to be.

Once we accept the rules at a gut level, they lead us out of negative restraint into positive freedom. By following a few simple guidelines, we become free from slavery to compulsive overeating and self-centered confusion.

Thank You for Your guidelines.

Twenty-Four Hours a Day

We practice the OA principles in all our affairs, twenty-four hours a day. Ours is not a diet program but a way of life. When we were eating compulsively, food occupied the central place in our lives every day. Abstinence replaces food as our prime concern, and maintaining abstinence means working the program.

When we do this, we are amazed at how well the day goes. Our work is easier and more productive. We spend less time and energy hassling with ourselves and other people. Best of all, we do not always have to be right. Being able to admit mistakes delivers us from egocentricity.

Being straight with ourselves enables us to be straight with others, and they in turn respond more positively. We are less concerned that everyone like us and more concerned about growth in the program. By placing principles before personalities, we get less snarled up in confused, game-playing relationships.

May You be foremost in my mind, twenty-four hours a day.

Stop Overeating, Start Living

Physical abstinence is just the beginning of the new life which OA offers to us. When our Higher Power controls our life, we become free of the mental obsession with food. Then we are able to get down to the business of living which we avoided with our illness.

Rather than reaching out with both hands to grab and hold on to all we can get, we begin to think in terms of giving and serving. We may start by sharing what OA has done for us with newcomers to the program. It is the newcomer who is our reminder of who we were and where we came from.

We find that though we can never eat spontaneously, we can live much more spontaneously than before. Because we feel less guilt and fear, we can experience the joy of acting from the center of our being. Knowing that our Higher Power is in control, we have trust and faith that the results of our actions will be okay. Each day becomes less of a trial and more of an opportunity.

Today, may I experience the spontaneity that comes with Your control.

Friends and Enemies

Sometimes our friends or members of our family urge us to eat food that is not part of our plan. If we allow ourselves to be manipulated into eating something to please someone else, we are in danger of losing the most important thing in our life—abstinence. Anyone who tries to make us feel uncomfortable because of our illness is acting as an enemy, rather than a friend.

To some people close to us, an explanation of our food plan may be helpful. Repeated discussions, however, are usually unnecessary and unproductive. We alone are responsible for what we put into our mouths. If those around us cannot or will not understand, then that is their problem, not ours.

When confronted with food which we know is harmful to us, the simplest response is a firm "No, thank you." When we ourselves are determined to maintain abstinence, no one else, whether friend or enemy, can prevent us from following our plan.

Protect me, Lord, from my friends and enemies.

Too Thin?

After losing weight, we may find ourselves being told that we are getting too thin. Often, the people who tell us this are not particularly thin themselves. Their comments are obstensibly made out of concern for our health, but it is more likely that they arise out of envy. Another reason could be the commenter's own personal fear of losing weight. Then, too, a thin person will sometimes feel threatened when we, who were formerly fat, come down to normal weight.

Whatever the reason, it is not the responsibility of anyone else to tell us how much we should or should not weigh. We alone are responsible for our own body.

When we turn our will and our life over to the care of our Higher Power, our body is included. The God who creates us will show us how he intends our body to look. We do not need to be concerned or swayed by the remarks of those who may not have our best interests at heart.

I trust You to take care of my body.

Sponsors

Most of us never outgrow our need for a sponsor. Someone who has had similar experiences can give us the understanding which we require in order to continue to grow in the program. A sponsor who maintains current, clean abstinence and who seriously works the program is someone who inspires us to follow. We could not control our disease by ourselves. As we recover, we continue to need help.

With a food sponsor, we can discuss our particular menus and problems. When we make a mistake, we need to share it with another person in order to profit from it and put it behind us. A program sponsor gives us encouragement and insight as we work the steps. When we are maintaining our desired weight, a maintenance sponsor helps us make any necessary adjustments. Sponsorship is one of the most important OA tools, and we are foolish if we do not take advantage of it. Alone, we are powerless over food.

Thank You for sponsors.

The Pause That Refreshes

For strength, we are learning to lean on our Higher Power instead of food. We have undoubtedly taken many "breaks" which involved ingesting one or another addictive substance. Instead of making us stronger, those substances eventually made us weaker. Thanks to OA, we are finding a dependable source of refreshment.

Starting the day with a few minutes of contact with God enables us to draw from His strength that which we need. Throughout the day, when we become weary or perplexed or pressured, we can pause to renew that contact. It is a constant source of Power whenever we open ourselves to it.

Allowing ourselves to become too busy is asking for trouble. We can concentrate actively for only so long without a period of rest and relaxation. Frequent time out each day to consult with our Higher Power makes our work more effective and our leisure more creative.

I seek Your presence, Lord.

I Am a Compulsive Overeater

The one fact which I need to remember constantly is that I am a compulsive overeater. If I forget it, I will eventually break my abstinence. There is no way that I can eat "normally," like most other people. I either eat according to my OA plan or I eat very abnormally, according to my compulsion.

Because I am a compulsive overeater, I do not take tastes of this or that, and I do not have snacks. I have found from sad experience that this kind of uncontrolled eating is impossible for me to handle. I know that I need to plan every day the three measured meals which I will eat.

Because of the new life that OA has given to me, I am grateful for my disease. Without it, I would not have found the measure of peace and serenity which comes to me every day as I work the program.

May I remember that I am a compulsive overeater.

Amends To Ourselves

By our compulsive overeating, we ourselves have usually been hurt more than anyone else. Because we could not trust ourselves, we had little self-respect or self-confidence. In many cases, we actually hated ourselves for what we thought was weakness and now know to be a disease.

By ourselves, we cannot control the illness, but through OA and our Higher Power, we are able to recover. With recovery comes a new attitude toward self. We see that we find happiness by abstaining from compulsive overeating and seeking each day to do God's will. New power and order enter into our daily activities, and we begin to approve of ourselves.

The best way that we can make amends to ourselves for self-hate and failure to develop our abilities is by maintaining our abstinence each day. We then gain the confidence to say "no" to those things which are not in our best interest. Instead of destroying ourselves with too much food and the wrong kind of activities, we are building a new life fed with the nourishment from our Higher Power.

Thank You for new opportunities to grow.

Amends To Others

The people most affected by our disease were undoubtedly the members of our own family. Then came our closest friends, if we had any when we were overeating. These people were directly affected by our negative moods and by our withdrawal away from them into overeating. They also may have been affected by not getting food which should have been theirs, but which we had eaten. Some of us stole money to buy food that we did not need but had to have. Some of us stole food.

Making amends is sometimes embarrassing and often difficult. It involves much pride-swallowing. A simple, sincere apology may be all that is necessary. There may be concrete acts which we can perform. As with making amends to ourselves, the best way we can make up for the hurt we have caused to family and friends is by abstaining from compulsive overeating. As we abstain, we reach out to those around us instead of withdrawing. Our own sanity is the best gift we can give to others.

May I have the courage to make amends.

Listening

As we learn to listen to our Higher Power, we also learn to listen with more awareness to ourselves and others. Being willing to spend time alone, in quiet, is essential to listening. We often fear silence and being alone, and we escape into distractions and busy-work.

Prayer is not so much telling and asking as it is listening. Prayer in this sense may be practiced continually during the day. By taking Step Three, we are giving up our will and becoming receptive to the will of our Higher Power. We focus less on our egotistical concerns and more on God, as we understand Him. That understanding grows through listening.

By listening, we become aware of needs, feelings, and responses within ourselves which we had previously ignored. Knowing ourselves better, we are more direct and honest with others and more responsive to them. The communication which develops with our Higher Power is on a level deep enough to relate us more meaningfully to everyone around us.

I will listen today to Your voice.

Praying Only . . .

In Step Eleven, we are "praying only for knowledge of His will for us and the power to carry that out." How that simplifies our prayer! We do not have to worry about asking for the right things in the right way. We simply pray that we may know God's will and be given the power to do it.

This Step is closely related to Step Three, since we are leaving the decisions up to God. He knows better than we what is best for us to have and to do. We make ourselves available to His direction without attaching conditions and clauses about what we will and will not do.

This kind of prayer frees us from much worry and anxiety. We accept abstinence as God's will for us, since without abstinence we are powerless to do much of anything. Beyond that, we are prepared to live each day as our Higher Power gives it to us, trusting that He will show us His will and supply us with the power that we need.

This is my prayer, Lord.

Carrying the Message

We do not keep our program unless we give it away. Our participation in meetings is a means of sharing with others what OA has given us. We are genuinely interested in newcomers, because they remind us of where we came from and because they give us an opportunity to strengthen our own program by sharing what we have received.

Sometimes we carry the message by providing transportation for someone who otherwise would not get to a meeting. Sometimes we give of ourselves by simply listening when a newcomer needs to talk. Practicing the OA principles in all areas of our life is carrying the message, even to those who are not compulsive overeaters.

Abstinence and the OA program now occupy the central place in our lives, the place which was once held by food. Following the will of our Higher Power means that we carry the message as He directs us. We are willing to be used in whatever way God moves us to give away our program.

May I serve You by carrying the message.

September 13

Hungering

Deep within us is a hunger which is not satisfied by food. We hunger for love and fellowship with each other and we hunger for communion with our Higher Power. We were not made to be alone and isolated. Withdrawing into compulsive overeating makes the deep hunger even worse.

As long as we are alive, we will never be fully satisfied. There will always be more love to give and receive and more steps to take on our spiritual journey. In this sense, we will always be hungry. Spiritual hunger is a good thing, as long as we recognize it for what it is and do not try to appease it with material substitutes.

Our Higher Power has created us with a hunger which He alone can satisfy. As our progress through the Twelve Steps brings us closer to Him and closer to each other, we experience a fulfillment which we had not known before. We are learning to hunger for spirituality.

Bless our hunger, we pray.

Emptiness

When we were overeating, we felt empty inside no matter how much we ate. Now that we are abstaining, we may still experience periods of feeling empty. This emptiness is especially likely to occur after an occasion to which we have looked forward with much anticipation.

Perhaps we expect too much from a person or an event and feel let down when reality falls short of our anticipation. Perhaps we find ourselves with a group of people where conversation is superficial and relationships are phony. Putting on a mask and keeping it in place for any length of time leaves us feeling drained and empty.

Without honest, meaningful contact with other people, we are emotionally undernourished. In order to have the mutually-nurturing relationships we need, our false fronts have to be abandoned. Through this program, we learn to seek out the kinds of people and activities that fill us and to avoid those that leave us empty.

Fill my emptiness, Lord.

Peace

Our mental obsession with food gave us little peace. The refined sugars and carbohydrates which we craved left us jangled and over-stimulated. Our guilt and self-hate kept us in a state of fear and turmoil. We raced about frantically in our minds trying to think of a way out of our misery.

Abstaining from refined sugar and carbohydrates gives us physical peace. Our body is no longer in an uproar; it is functioning calmly and efficiently. The Twelve Steps of recovery free us from the mental obsession with food and bring about emotional and spiritual peace. The more control we relinquish to our Higher Power, the more peace He gives us.

The peace which comes through working our program is not stagnant—it is rich and creative. It is the peace which results from an ordered life and confidence in God. Instead of going in circles, both physically and mentally, we move in measured progress along the path which our Higher Power shows us step by step each day.

Thank You for peace.

Understanding

The understanding which we gain through the OA program is a source of constant amazement and gratitude. First, we begin to understand our illness. Then, we grow in understanding of ourselves and others. Finally, our eyes are opened more and more to the spiritual aspects of our existence.

Hearing someone else's story gives us insight into our own behavior. We act as mirrors, reflecting each other's problems and solutions. As we act, we are given greater understanding of why we do what we do and how we may function better. In order to gain more understanding, we must first act on the knowledge we have. Intellectual awareness alone will not enable us to control our disease.

The empathy and understanding which we receive from fellow OA members gives us the strength and hope to recover. We begin to see where our attitudes were wrong and how to go about correcting them. As we acknowledge the Power greater than ourselves and give our lives over to Him, we open a new channel of spiritual insight and understanding.

May I understand.

God Is Here

The Power which restores us to sanity is not something remote and abstract which we must search for by reading books and performing great feats. Our Higher Power is with us constantly and is involved in the minute details of every day. We do not have to wait and work to become acceptable to God. He accepts us now, just as we are.

What gets in the way of our awareness of God is self. If we are narrowly focused on the concerns of ego and self-will, we ignore the presence of a Higher Power. Then we become weak and confused in our aloneness.

To be aware of the presence of God in our lives every day, all we need is the willingness to be open to Him. We find that He is indeed "closer than breathing and nearer than hands and feet." What we may have spent years searching for or denying turns out to be the ground of our existence and the Power that sustains us every minute.

Increase my awareness of You, I pray.

Bad Days

There are some days when we wake up in the morning knowing with a sixth sense that the day is going to be a hard one. These are the days when it is difficult to get out of bed, when we would prefer not to face whatever awaits us. There is no way around these days; we must get through them the best way we can.

Our most useful tool for coping with a bad day is abstinence. Nothing is impossible when we are abstaining from compulsive overeating. Often our problem lies not in the external events of the day but in recognizing a part of ourself that has been hidden and repressed. We resist facing honestly what our Higher Power is revealing to us about our inner life.

When we are determined not to escape into food, we will come out of a bad day stronger than we were before. We reinforce our new way of living, which is to turn difficult situations over to our Higher Power and then act as He guides us, step by step.

May I be closer to You during the bad days.

Know Yourself

The OA program fosters self-knowledge on a practical, physical level as well as on the more abstract emotional and intellectual levels. We come to know what foods we can handle comfortably, how we can arrange our day so that we do not get exhausted, which people we need to avoid if we are to maintain our serenity.

We had so little self-confidence when we were overeating that we were inclined to accept other people's ideas of who we were and what we should do. By trying to be and do what others expected, we may have lost sight of our inner selves. The emptiness caused by not knowing and respecting ourselves led in turn to more overeating as we tried to fill the inner void with food.

Self-knowledge requires courage and honesty. It involves admitting our weaknesses and mistakes, rather than pretending to be perfect. As we come to know ourselves—our preferences, needs, and goals—we gain strength and integrity. The Power greater than ourselves gives us the insight to know who we are physically, emotionally, and spiritually.

Thank You for self-knowledge.

A New Self-Image

As we lose weight, our self-image needs to change along with our body. We may have had a mental image of ourself as a thin person, but this image probably did not go beyond the physical. If we continue to think of ourself as the same confused, compulsive, childish person we once were, we are not facilitating our emotional and spiritual growth.

The OA program gives us the power to become a new person. If we see ourselves as daily growing more sane, more serene, more confident, reality will reflect our inner vision.

Perhaps the most important change in our self-image involves our relationship to our Higher Power. Before, we probably saw ourselves as the center of our world and devoted our energies to protecting and building up our fragile ego. We were all alone in an unfriendly world. Now, we see ourselves as God's creation, subject to His purpose and plan. As we yield to His authority and accept His love, we find strength, security, and peace. By losing ourselves, we find ourselves.

Create in me a new self-image.

Trusting Gut Reactions

Since we could not trust ourselves where food was concerned, we had trouble trusting ourselves in all aspects of life. We became divided internally and unsure of what we thought or how we felt or how we should act. We may have depended on other people to tell us what we liked, what to do, and how to do it.

It is with a great sense of joy that we become aware of our own individuality and preferences. If we experience a negative gut reaction to a certain person or activity, then we need to examine our reasons for continuing the relationship or activity. We do not have to like everyone, nor do we have to do everything. The sooner we become selective, the more we develop as individuals and the more integrity we possess. If we continually force ourselves to do things which violate our inner integrity, then we are frustrated and growth is slow.

Gut reactions need to be examined calmly and intelligently. They are there to tell us something about ourselves.

Give me a healthy respect for my gut reactions.

Scales

During our dieting days, we probably spent much time getting on and off the scales. In OA, we are advised not to weigh more than once a month. Though we want to get rid of excess weight, we do not want to be obsessed with pounds and ounces. This program involves much more than weight control, and to make the scales our ultimate judge is to miss the mark.

If we are honestly abstaining from compulsive overeating and working our program, we will lose weight. The rate of loss will vary from person to person and from week to week. Even, and especially, when the scale registers what we want it to register, we continue to honestly abstain and work the OA program.

In OA, we are more concerned with the progress we make in controlling our disease than we are with our specific weight on any particular day. If our illness is under control, weight control will follow. Scales are useful for measuring physical progress, but they are not a god.

May I use the scales wisely.

Positive Leads

As our serenity grows, the clamor and confusion inside our heads die down. Instead of being pulled in many different directions and uncertain of which way to turn, we gradually discern the positive voice that leads us forward. Rather than trying to analyze all possible alternatives intellectually, we gain the confidence to choose the positive way without agonizing indecision.

To worry and speculate about the roads not taken is counter-productive and wasteful of our energies. We pray that we may know the will of our Higher Power for us, and then we act according to the best of our knowledge. The more we practice listening to the still, small voice within, the more positive direction we will receive.

The mental calmness which we experience as we abstain from compulsive overeating clears away our former confusion. We may make mistakes, but as long as we can admit them and stay in contact with our Higher Power, we will continue to follow His positive leads.

Keep me on Your positive path.

Accepting Where We Are

Wherever we are when we come to this program is where we begin. Some of us have farther to go along the road to self-actualization than others. No one of us ever arrives in this life. There is always more work to be done.

Believing that our Higher Power has a plan for each of us, we accept the place where He has put us right now. We do not expect to stay in this place, but it is a necessary part of our growth and development. We cannot move on until we understand where we are now and how we got here.

Our Fourth Step inventory gives us an opportunity to examine past actions which have led to our current situation. We may not like what we discover, but an honest appraisal of our weaknesses and faults as well as our strengths is preparation for constructive change. Accepting where we are frees us from morbid obsession with the past and enables us to move on into the future.

May I accept where I am as the best place for me to be today.

Don't Hang On

As long as we are alive, we will experience times of joy and times of sadness. Trying to hang on to the periods of elation and avoid the inevitable depression which each of us feels from time to time causes us to seek artificial stimulation. Using food to try to stay on cloud nine did not work, and neither does anything else.

By turning over our lives, we become willing to let go and move through the periods of joy and sadness as we come to them. Trying to hang on arrests our progress. Nothing is certain in this life except change, and when we stop over-eating we are better able to deal with the variations in our feelings and circumstances.

Whatever our current mood or situation, we can remain abstinent. Abstinence gives our lives stability and order, in spite of changes. Being centered in the Power greater than ourselves keeps us from being overly affected by either elation or depression.

By focusing on You, may I move calmly through the times of joy and the times of sadness.

Character Defects

Beginning the OA program, we are inclined to feel that our problems and difficulties are largely due to circumstances and other people. The enemy seems to be outside. The more we work the Steps, the more we realize that our troubles are within, rather than without. Furthermore, we learn that the only person we can change is ourself.

We see that the root of our difficulty lies in being centered on self instead of centered in our Higher Power. Our egos can take us only so far before we reach a point where continued growth demands that we begin to abandon them. What a relief to get rid of the anxiety, frustration, and fear that goes with an ego-centered life!

Our Higher Power removes our character defects as we become willing to let go of them. Honest awareness is our first task, and this is facilitated by maintaining abstinence from compulsive overeating. Abstinence gives us the honesty and the energy to change. As we change, circumstances and relationships improve.

I ask that You remove my character defects according to Your will.

We Admit

Three of the Twelve Steps have to do with admitting. We admit that we are powerless over food and cannot manage our own lives; we admit our wrongs to God, ourselves, and another person; we continue to take inventory and admit when we are wrong.

Out of honest admission of our weakness comes strength. We are able to see ourselves realistically and with clarity. When we are humble enough to admit our wrongs, we get rid of the false front we had tried to maintain. This frees us to be who we are, without pretense.

When we admit our faults, we are cleansed. We no longer have to try to hide and cover up our weaknesses and mistakes. Instead of pretending to be perfect, we can be human and satisfied with progress.

We admit that we have a progressive disease, and we learn how to control it. We do not pretend to ourselves or others that we can eat like everyone else, because we are compulsive overeaters. We cannot manage our own lives, but there is One who can.

I admit that I am powerless, and I am grateful for Your Power in my life.

My Own Body

My body is where I live. Its size and shape is a matter between me and my Higher Power. No one else is responsible for my body. In the past, I may have permitted other people to influence what I ate and how much I weighed, but I now take full responsibility.

Other people may think that I am too fat or too thin, but that is their problem, not mine. I am learning what my body needs in order to operate at peak efficiency. I am learning to avoid the foods which I do not handle well. What and how much I eat depends on my own preference and the requirements of my metabolism.

My body is a gift to me from my Higher Power. Maintaining it in the best possible condition is my response to God's gift. No one else can tell me how best to maintain my body, since no one else is living in it or receives its inner signals. If I honestly interpret the signals which come from my body, I will stay abstinent and healthy.

Thank You for my body.

The Satisfaction of Work

Using our God-given talents and abilities to do the work He assigns us brings deep satisfaction. Many of us used to eat a lot of "idle bread" which we did not need. Now that we are eating less, we find that we derive satisfaction from working more.

Work is an opportunity to give away the gifts we are given. It is a sharing which requires effort and discipline. If we do not work up to our maximum level of ability, our satisfaction is reduced. As we give away our gifts, we are given more.

Maintaining abstinence improves the quality of our work and increases our output. Instead of doing just enough to get by, we are challenged to give the best that we have. Abstaining from compulsive overeating can give us the courage and confidence to change jobs when necessary.

When we are emotionally upset, turning to a task which absorbs us physically or mentally or both can have a healing effect. Rather than a curse, work can be a blessing, especially when we realize that ultimately we are working with and for our Higher Power.

We give thanks for the satisfaction of work.

Perspective

When our vision was clouded by self-will, our perspective was narrow and subjective. We saw people and events only as they fostered or frustrated our egotistical concerns. The world was a frightening place, since we thought that our welfare was entirely dependent on our own efforts.

Coming to believe in a Higher Power gives us a new, broader perspective. We learn the security of trusting eternal values and moral principles. When we pray only for knowledge of God's will for us and the power to carry that out, we begin to see ourselves as serving rather than surviving. Particular acts may or may not be successful from our point of view, but we can move on in confidence, knowing that our past, present, and future is in His hands.

The new perspective which comes to us as we work the OA program enables us to accept defeats as well as successes and irritations as well as satisfactions. All experience is for our growth and development.

Create in us a new perspective.

Being True

Without rigorous honesty, we do not recover from compulsive overeating. We need to be honest about what we eat and honest about how we feel. In the past, we covered up pain with sugar frosting and tried to drown our inadequacies in carbohydrates. The time has come to deal with truth.

Alone, we are not perceptive enough to see the truth, nor strong enough to bear it. It is through our Higher Power and the OA fellowship that we are able to become true to the best that is in us. We admit that we have been living falsely, and we turn over our muddled lives so that God may straighten them out. His spirit is truth, and the light of that truth is what we need for our recovery.

Our Higher Power shows us how to be true step by step, as we are ready to progress. Each day we become more in touch with our real selves and each day our strength increases. Being true sets us free from compulsive overeating and free from the false values, hopes, and expectations which have inhibited us.

Lead me into truth.

The Power of Faith

A very small amount of faith is all that is required to begin the OA program. Hearing the stories of those who have changed and found new life gives us faith in the program. Coming to the limit of our resources makes us willing to try believing in a Higher Power, or at least acting as if we believed.

Sometimes we resist believing because deep down we do not want to change. When we honestly want to stop eating compulsively more than we want anything else, we will be given the necessary faith.

Faith grows as we work the program. As we see results, we are encouraged to keep trying in spite of setbacks. When we are able to stop eating compulsively through OA and our Higher Power, we come to believe that we can succeed in other areas of life, as well. Faith spreads to include other accomplishments which before had seemed impossible. Through the power of faith, we are able to become all that God intends us to be.

May our faith grow daily.

Being Committed

Success comes with commitment. We cannot maintain abstinence, or a marriage, or a profession, or anything else without being committed to it. Genuine commitment is the attitude required of us if we are to benefit from OA. The program is not something we pick up and put down when we feel like it. If abstinence is not the most important thing in our lives, we will not be able to maintain it.

Sharing our commitment out loud, with another person, reinforces it. We need to stay in contact with our OA friends. It is during the busy times that we especially need to remember our priorities. A phone call plugs us in to the group strength which sustains our individual efforts.

The physical, emotional, and spiritual benefits which come to us every day as we abstain and work the Twelve Steps are what nourish us. Being committed to the OA program is our strength and our recovery.

Make firm my commitment to Your way.

Friendship

Through this program, we learn that we have choices. Not only can we choose what we will eat and what we will do, but also we can choose our friends. As we become honest, unaddicted people, we are able to relate to each other on a level of mutuality and admiration rather than out of dependency and fear. We gain the self-confidence to choose those with whom we enjoy spending time and sharing, rather than slavishly catering to anyone who will notice us.

Friends in OA have a special bond, since we share a common problem and a common solution. By putting principles before personalities, we avoid dependency and childish demands. Though we love and support each other, we do not cling together, since we are each dependent on a Higher Power. Our friends give us the gift of themselves, which shows us who we are.

Thank You for friendship.

Being Before Doing

What we are comes before what we do. In order to produce good fruit, the tree has to be a good tree. If we are not whole, integrated, and in touch with ourselves and our Higher Power, the actions that we take will not be satisfying.

For us compulsive overeaters, being abstinent is more important than anything we do. When we are abstinent, all things are possible. We still have to make choices, deal with frustration and conflict, and accept some defeats, but we are coping with reality rather than escaping.

The best things that we do are those which our Higher Power does through us. Our role is to be ready and available, a sharpened tool which He may use. Often we do not see the ultimate results of our actions. We trust that what we do will be acceptable and according to His will.

May I be what You intend.

Staying With God

God never forsakes us; we forsake Him. We become so involved in our concerns and activities that we forget to open our eyes and our hearts to His presence. We may be physically abstinent, but still allow food to have the most important place in our lives. If our Higher Power is not at the center of our lives, we will find it difficult (if not impossible) to be emotionally abstinent.

Emotional binges occur when we wander away from our Higher Power into self-centered preoccupation. Without His control, we lose our serenity. There will always be causes of conflict and frustration in our daily lives. How we handle these situations depends on our spiritual condition.

By ourselves, we cannot manage our own lives. Our behavior can be insane. It is through the Power greater than ourselves that we are led into order, sanity, and recovery. To stay with this Power is our salvation.

May we not forsake You.

Old Anxieties

The causes of our past anxieties may no longer be operative. Compulsive eating behavior, however, brings back these anxieties in full force. Our weight may be normal, but we are never safe from the danger of personality disintegration brought on by a return, however slight, to compulsive overeating habits.

If we are to maintain our sanity and our sobriety, we must continue to abstain completely from all patterns of thinking and behavior associated with overeating. We have become new people. Daily we grow stronger and freer from old fears and anxieties. The new behavior which gives us this new freedom is abstinence. Without abstinence, we will again be overwhelmed and incapacitated by irrational fear and anxiety.

To be alive is to experience a certain amount of anxiety. We will never be completely rid of all fear. As long as we are abstaining, however, and relying on our Higher Power instead of ourselves, we will be given the confidence and serenity we need.

I turn over to You my anxieties.

Learning From Mistakes

We can learn from our mistakes so that we do not have to make the same ones over and over again. If a particular attitude or situation consistently makes it difficult for us to follow our food plan, then that attitude or situation needs to be changed. Slips do not just happen. They indicate that something is wrong with our program and that we have not yet learned what we need to know about ourselves.

Being aware of the circumstances which make us vulnerable to overeating helps us to be prepared for temptation and to find ways to avoid it wherever possible. If there are certain foods which we cannot resist, then we should not have those foods available. If trying to do too much makes us tired and emotionally upset, then we need to be less ambitious and learn to delegate responsibility. Compulsive overeating or emotional bingeing indicates that we are not living in a way which satisfies our basic needs.

Lord, may we learn from our mistakes.

Abstinence, Not Punishment

By abstaining from compulsive overeating, we are doing ourselves the biggest favor imaginable. We are literally saving our lives, physically, emotionally, and spiritually. We should never think of abstinence as punishment. Eating too much food and the wrong kind of food was the real punishment.

Each day we plan three attractive meals consisting of foods which we enjoy. We do not exaggerate our efforts to make the meals enjoyable, since we do not want to reactivate our former obsession with food. At the same time, we choose foods which appeal to us and do not punish ourselves with boring, unappetizing menus.

The refined sugars and carbohydrates with which we rewarded ourselves in the past are no longer a reward but poison to our systems. Overeating any food punishes us through loss of both control and peace of mind. We maintain abstinence from compulsive overeating in order to take care of ourselves and feel good.

By Your grace, may I maintain abstinence.

Powerless

I am powerless over food. By myself, I am unable to control what I eat or manage my life. Thanks to OA, I have found a Higher Power by which I am learning to live a new life.

So that this Higher Power may live in me, I surrender myself. No longer do I try to live by my own efforts; no longer do I try by myself to control what I eat. Since I am powerless over food and cannot manage my life, I give myself to God as I understand Him and ask that He live through me.

When I surrender, my Higher Power takes over. Then, instead of being weak and powerless, I become strong through His strength. So very simple. I wonder why it takes so long to learn? The only requirement is, in the words of T. S. Eliot, "a condition of complete simplicity, costing not less than everything." [1]

May I remember that without You, I am powerless.

[1] T. S. Eliot, "Little Gidding."

Feeling Deprived

If I allow myself to feel deprived, sooner or later I will overeat or react with negative emotions. I am a human being, a child of God with the same rights as all of His other children. I have needs and preferences which, if denied and repressed, will surface in a destructive way.

If those around me are eating a special meal and I eat leftovers which I do not particularly like, I will feel deprived. I may become bad-tempered and I may overeat later to compensate. I do not need to have what others are eating, if it is not on my food plan, but my meal should be pleasing to me. I do not need to have and do what everyone else has and does, but I can recognize my desires and preferences and satisfy them when doing so does not injure anyone else.

By overeating, I deprived myself of good health, peace of mind, self-respect, an attractive appearance. By abstaining, I am making amends to myself for that deprivation. By working the program, I am learning how to satisfy my legitimate needs.

I trust You to supply my needs.

Moving Forward

Time past is gone forever, and we can never go back to it. Even our disease progresses forward. We cannot expect to control it by a return to measures which may have worked for a time in the past. Those methods eventually failed, and trying them again will only bring us to the same point of failure.

The only way to avoid repetitious failure is to move forward creatively as our Higher Power leads us. Each day is a new creation, and each day brings new lessons and opportunities. We build on what is past, but we do not need to repeat it.

Moving forward involves risking what is unknown. The old, familiar rut, depressing as it is, is a known quantity. Moving out of it requires that we have courage and that we trust in One who knows and cares. To move on, we must act. Insights do not produce growth until they are accompanied by specific actions.

May I risk new actions as You lead me forward.

Rigorous Honesty

As we work the OA program, we find that we cannot be rigorously honest about what we are eating unless we are rigorously honest about our other actions as well. Once our Higher Power takes charge of our lives, a general housecleaning occurs. Gradually, we see that the attitudes and activities which undermine our integrity have to go.

The housecleaning process can be painful. It involves facing aspects of ourselves which we would prefer to remain hidden—our dependency, pride, selfishness, avarice. Sex and money are often areas where our attitudes and practices need revision. What we are doing is shifting from an ego-centered to a God-centered orientation, and the shift is not always smooth.

Rigorous honesty shows up harmful relationships for what they are. It illumines our motives, which are not always the best. The love and care of our Higher Power support us as our weaknesses are exposed. Through His healing power, we are strengthened and made whole.

Grant me the ability to practice rigorous honesty in all areas of my life.

Surrender

Continuing to take the first three Steps enables us to become increasingly surrendered to our Higher Power. Our goal is to let our egotistical selves be dissolved in a greater Self, so that the Higher Power lives through us. The loss of ego frightens us and attacks our illusions of self-sufficiency.

Here is where we can be grateful for our disease. If we were not convinced of our helplessness in the face of our obsession with food, we would not be desperate enough to surrender to a Higher Power. Only after we have tried and failed over and over again in our battle with compulsive overeating are we willing to accept the OA program.

We surrender in order to stop eating compulsively. We gain infinitely more than we had expected. Not only does our Higher Power give us abstinence from compulsive overeating, but more than that He gives us Himself. No longer do we live as an isolated, weak self, but in us lives the Power of the universe.

May we surrender completely to Your power.

Cutting Cords

Often we are bound in unhealthy ways to parents, husbands, wives, children, friends. When dependency and manipulation are masked as love, it is difficult to cut the cords that bind us. By ourselves we are unable to break free.

Listening to other compulsive overeaters helps us to see ourselves and our own situation more objectively. Working the steps builds emotional and spiritual maturity. Abstaining from compulsive overeating gives us the perception we need to see unhealthy relationships for what they are. Our growing self-respect motivates us to make changes.

We ate because we were too weak to face our problems. Now that we see where we have been manipulated and where we have manipulated others, we need the strength to cut the cords of unhealthy dependency. This strength comes from our Higher Power. Since we recognize our complete dependency on Him, we are no longer weakened by pseudo-dependencies on those close to us. We learn to relate to them positively, out of God's strength rather than our own weakness.

By Your power, may I cut the cords that bind me.

Admitting Wrongs

Step Ten reminds us to continue to take daily inventory and to promptly admit when we are wrong. By admitting our mistake out loud to the person we have harmed, we clear away bad feelings and guilt. The relationship is healed, and we are able to put the error behind us. Admitting that we are wrong helps us even more than the person we have injured.

Since it usually takes two people to disrupt a relationship, the entire blame may not be ours. Admitting our share of wrong, however, relieves us of guilt and opens the way to reconciliation.

Being able to apologize simply and sincerely means that we are not bound by pride and egotism. We do not always have to be right. By accepting our human fallibility, we are free to be ourselves, to make mistakes, to correct them, and to make amends.

Admitting wrongs keeps us honest with ourselves, with others, and with our Higher Power. We stay anchored in the real world and we practice healthy humility.

May I not be too proud to admit I am wrong.

Seeking the Best

We will never be satisfied with less than the best. When we were overeating, we may have settled for less than we were capable of being and achieving, but we were not happy about it. There is something in each of us that hungers for maximum growth and development.

When we stop drugging ourselves with food, we become aware of new possibilities and areas of growth. By controlling our disease, we release potential that had been buried under our obsession. As we come to know our Higher Power through this program, our appetite for the best is reawakened. Though we realize we will never achieve perfection, we are challenged to be and do the best that we can, just for today.

Lives that are committed to the care of God are directed by the best force there is. Only by dedication to knowing and doing His will is our search satisfied.

We seek You, Lord.

Relying on God

As compulsive overeaters, we relied on food to pick us up, calm us down, console us, excite us, help us, and sustain us. Since food was inadequate to do all of these things, we had to eat more and more until we became physically and emotionally addicted.

Recovery from our disease requires that dependency on food be replaced by dependency on a Higher Power. Only God, as each of us understands Him, is capable of supporting us at all times and in all situations. Food simply will not work. If we are not controlled by our Higher Power, we will be controlled by our addiction to compulsive overeating.

At first, we find it difficult to rely on a Power we cannot see. Our materialistic orientation makes us distrustful of the things that are of the spirit. Gradually, we come to believe as we witness the work of God through OA. We see evidence of His activity in our own lives, and we sense the peace and security that He gives. Reliance on God is our strength.

I depend on You for recovery.

To Abstain Is To Live

If we do not abstain from compulsive overeating, we do not live—we merely survive. Without abstinence, joy and creativity fade and we are left with only the effort of getting from one day to the next. We remember the despair of living without the OA program, and we are grateful that we have been given a reprieve from our former misery.

Abstaining is what we do each day in order to live the life our Higher Power intends us to have. There are good days and bad days and mediocre days. As long as we abstain from compulsive overeating, we are able to accept our passing moods and the events of each day with inner serenity. We make progress in our activities and in our understanding. We are alive to the possibilities of each moment.

To abstain requires that we choose a long-term satisfaction rather than a short-lived indulgence. To abstain is to walk with our Higher Power in the way He shows us.

Thank You for the power to abstain.

Physical Restraint

Self-control is hard work. When the urge comes to do something which we know is not in our best interest, we physically restrain ourselves from performing the destructive action. This often requires hard, physical effort.

We may want to eat when we should not be eating, we may want to lash out in anger, we may want to retreat from a difficult task, we may want to continue a harmful relationship. Whatever the urge, if we know deep down that it is contrary to God's will for us, we need to control it and not act on it.

Time spent with our Higher Power each day builds the strength and integrity which can control our destructive urges. Alone, we are powerless, but with the OA program supporting us we find strength we never had before. With abstinence comes the clarity of mind necessary to evaluate our urges and desires.

May I have the moral strength to physically restrain myself when necessary.

New Memories

If certain times of the year and certain activities are associated in our minds with overeating, we need to create new memories to blot out the old ones. If we are hung up on past loves, hates, and hurts, we need to let go of them so that we can live in the present.

Old eating habits keep alive old wounds and frustrations. Even after we have maintained abstinence for a significant length of time, we may be troubled by unresolved conflicts from the past. The fact that we are abstaining from compulsive overeating gives us a chance to see the problems more clearly and to then walk away from them when we have done all that we can do to resolve them.

The past and the future are in the hands of our Higher Power. If we work our program now and live the best we can today, we are creating good memories which will sustain us in the days to come.

Take charge of my memories, Lord.

Healing

God, as understood by each of us, has the Power to heal our bodies, minds, and hearts. Once we realize that we are sick, we can open ourselves to the Power which will effect our recovery. As we delve more deeply into the OA program, we see that it is not only the body which suffers from the disease of compulsive overeating. Mind and emotions are also muddled and in need of God's cleansing.

The healing process can be painful. Sometimes we have to get worse in order to get better. Sometimes we have to be more devastated by overeating, by pride, by fear and selfishness before we are willing to turn ourselves over to our Higher Power for healing. We do not make the effort to work the Twelve Steps until we see how desperately ill we are.

God heals, but He requires our cooperation and effort. The extent of our recovery is determined by the intensity of our desire to get well. When our desire is focused on the source of health and held there steadily, we can become whole.

We pray for healing.

Tomorrow Is Another Day

As compulsive overeaters, we can be tormented by the urge to finish everything right now, today. That was the way we used to eat, and it may still be the way we try to operate in other areas of behavior. It is possible to exchange our addiction to food for an addiction to work or perfection.

Trying to do everything today is just another example of self-will run riot. We are not superpeople and we cannot perform miracles. It is our Higher Power who makes possible our accomplishments, and His work is done slowly and gradually. God never expects more of us than we are able to deliver. It is our own pride that entices us to tackle the impossible.

As long as we are alive, our work will not be finished. Each day we are given new tasks to do and new experiences to enjoy. What we do not complete today can be continued tomorrow, according to the will of our Higher Power.

I leave tomorrow's tasks for tomorrow.

Accepting God's Will

Disappointments and hurts can send us into an orgy of self-pity if we are not willing to accept them as part of our Higher Power's plan. We do not understand why we must suffer disappointments and frustrations, but trusting God means that we accept our share of this world's pain.

When we look back on former disappointments, we are often able to see that what we so desperately wanted at the time would not have been the best thing for us. Our vision and judgment is limited. Faith that God is managing our lives according to His purposes can relieve us of unnecessary hurt and frustration.

To accept God's will is not to passively absorb all that happens to us like an inert sponge. It is to actively seek knowledge of His plan for our lives and to purposefully work according to the knowledge we receive. Acceptance is positive and cooperative.

Your will is what I seek to accept.

Abstaining From Harmful Relationships

Habit sometimes locks us into relationships which are not in our best interest. It is easy to mistake dependency for love. When we stop overeating compulsively, we can evaluate our attachments to other people with greater clarity and perception than was possible when we continually escaped into food.

Our OA friends act as sounding boards for us as we try to sort out the healthy from the unhealthy relationships in our lives. We may find that for our continued growth we need to move away from old emotional entanglements which are hampering our progress with the program. Abstaining from a harmful relationship can be as difficult at first as abstaining from compulsive overeating! The same physical restraint is necessary to keep ourselves from following old habit patterns.

By taking Step Three, we make all of our relationships with other people subject to the will of our Higher Power. When God comes first, other loves fall into their proper places.

Show me how to love.

Food Is Not Fun

We have used eating as a form of recreation and have looked for excitement in food. For years, we have associated food with fun. What we need to remember constantly is that uncontrolled eating is no longer fun for us, but a trip into anguish.

All of us have unpleasant memories of painful binges which began as attempts to experience pleasure through a small indulgence. We need to put these memories to work for us by associating them with the first compulsive bite. The idea that more and better food will bring us fun and pleasure is an illusion. We know this in our heads, but we need to feel it in our guts.

Food is nourishment for our bodies—nothing more. To experience pleasure with our minds and hearts and bodies, we open ourselves to richer interpersonal relationships, to aesthetic experiences, to sports and hobbies and work well done. Abstinence from compulsive overeating liberates us to enjoy the activities which *are* fun.

Thank You for the fun and joy which abstinence brings.

A Good Meal

A good meal for us is an abstinent meal. Fancy frills and gourmet delights are not good if they threaten our abstinence. Because we have over-emphasized food in the past, we tend to be too concerned about what we will have for dinner—and lunch—and breakfast.

It is a relief to come to the conclusion that whatever we have to eat is good if it fits our food plan. We do not have to spend a lot of time and energy deciding what we will eat today. If what we choose does not turn out to be especially pleasing, we are free to choose something else tomorrow.

Most of us are familiar with the basic principles of good nutrition. By abstaining from compulsive overeating, we are giving our bodies the best possible treatment. By avoiding refined sugars and starches, we eliminate empty calories and choose those foods with the protein, vitamins, and minerals necessary for good health. Whatever we eat, the abstinent meal is a good meal.

Thank You for good, abstinent meals.

Food Is Not Home

Breaking abstinence may be an attempt to go home emotionally. Since we associate food, and especially certain foods, with early experience, we may turn to food when we crave the emotional support of home.

Perhaps our early home life did not provide the emotional support and security we needed, causing us to attach a false significance to the food which we were given. The habit of turning to food and eating as a substitute for love, acceptance, and security may be deeply ingrained in our psyche. We may have come to depend on food instead of people to satisfy our emotional needs.

The problem is, of course, that food is not a satisfactory substitute for love and acceptance. However much we eat, the emotional satisfaction will be only temporary and soon disintegrate into despair and self-hatred. The home we crave can best be built here and now by working the OA program and loving the people our Higher Power gives us to love today.

May I realize that food is not home.

Truth

Overeating covered up the truth. We fed our illusions with food which harmed our bodies. The illusions grew bigger and stronger until our minds were fog-bound by the illusions instead of illuminated by truth.

Giving up our illusions is frightening and painful, but in the long run it is less difficult than trying to live with them and by them. It is impossible to get rid of our illusions by ourselves. The Higher Power leads us to truth by means of the Twelve Steps and the OA program. Abstinence from compulsive overeating is necessary in order to stop feeding our illusions and let the truth come through.

Knowing the truth sets us free. We no longer have to cling to old dependencies and self-defeating habits. Our Higher Power gives us as much truth as we are willing to work for and accept. We are not overwhelmed, but are gradually able to assimilate the reality of our situation. By accepting reality and refraining from using food as an escape, we are able to live with truth instead of illusions.

Lead me by the Power of truth.

Accent on the Present

When we were obsessed with food, we were often obsessed with the past as well. We would rehash old hurts and resentments, old fears and desires. Our dreams, along with our waking hours, may have been filled with people from our past. Such preoccupation with the past prevented us from focusing on the present.

By realizing that compulsive overeating is a non-stop trip back to the hurts of the past, we become more determined to maintain abstinence. If we are to be alive in the present, we need to let go of the past. What is over is over and cannot be replayed except in our minds.

What we can do is turn our memories over to our Higher Power for healing. The creative Spirit which is not bound by time can take away old hurts and resentments. Then we are free to deal with the present and concentrate on doing God's will for us now, today. Living in the present keeps us in touch with the Power which restores us to sanity.

May I remember that You are always now.

Gifts of the Spirit

Through the OA program, we come to desire spiritual gifts as well as material necessities. Experience shows us that serenity is priceless and something to be desired more than unnecessary food. Courage, wisdom, faith, hope, love, humility—these are all spiritual gifts which come to us from our Higher Power as we abstain and work our program.

As we receive these gifts of the spirit, we are able to share them with others. Giving them away to our families and friends insures that we will receive them more abundantly ourselves. We come to realize that a small gift of time and attention can mean more than an expensive material present.

God's gifts are available to us whenever we are open to receive them. By abstaining from compulsive overeating, we make our spirits ready to accept their rightful gifts.

I pray that I may be ready to accept Your spiritual gifts.

Food Is Not Love

With our heads, we know that food is not the same thing as love. When this fact sinks into our emotions, we are released from our obsession with food. In order to reach this point of emotional development, we need to abstain physically from compulsive overeating. As long as we are physically addicted to refined sugars and starches and binge foods, we do not have the perspective necessary to move away from our emotional attachment to these foods.

It is easy for babies and children to confuse food with love. As they mature, they learn to discriminate between the two. If we are compulsive overeaters, we need the OA program and a spiritual awakening to bring clarity to our confusion. We have much emotional and spiritual growing up to do.

If our early needs for love were not satisfied, no amount of food will compensate. It is by giving love that we are able to fill our inner emptiness, and it is through our Higher Power that we are healed and made able to love.

May we remember in our hearts that food is not love.

Fear of Giving

It is often the fear of rejection which makes us afraid to give of ourselves. The person who is reluctant to share at a meeting may be holding back because of this fear. To share is to reveal who we are and where we are. If we feel inadequate, we do not want to expose this imagined inadequacy to other people.

If our self-image is too grand and inflated, we cannot possibly live up to it in reality. Expecting ourselves to be perfect sets us up for frustration and fear, since we know deep down that we do not measure up to our image of perfection.

With humility comes the willingness to give of what we have and what we are right now, without waiting until we are more eloquent or more accomplished. What we have to share is what someone else needs to receive. By focusing more on the needs of others and less on the imaginary concept of ourselves which is our ego, we learn to overcome our fear of giving. What we have to give now is enough for today.

May I not be afraid to give.

Learning Moderation

If we had known how to practice moderation, we would not have become compulsive overeaters. Following the abstinence guidelines enables us to eat moderately. Working the Twelve Steps teaches us moderation in other activities.

Knowing when to quit involves knowing ourselves. We tend to get carried away with our determination to finish a job today, to explain our life history to a new friend in one afternoon, to complete a major project in record time. The tendency to devour life rapidly in huge chunks can be as damaging as compulsive overeating.

It is the serenity we acquire from contact with our Higher Power that saves us from wearing ourselves out compulsively. An awareness of the quiet Power and order which sustains all life calms our over-stimulated personalities. Dependence on God as we understand Him gives us the support and confidence to be content with moderate efforts and accomplishments.

Teach me to practice moderation.

How Much Is Enough?

We continue to weigh and measure our food when we are maintaining as well as when we are losing. Since we are compulsive overeaters, we do not have a built-in concept of how much food is enough. Exact measurements relieve us of the anxiety of deciding how much is enough. Since we are experts at rationalizing extra amounts, we do not allow ourselves to estimate portions when scales and measuring cups are available.

For the compulsive overeater, no amount of food is enough. We make a rational decision about our food plan for the day, basing the decision on the objective nutritional requirements of our body rather than subjective emotional cravings. We give this food plan to a qualified sponsor, which prevents us from getting lost in endless preoccupation and anxiety about what we are going to eat.

When we conscientiously follow the abstinence guidelines, we can rest secure in the knowledge that we have eaten the right amount of food.

May I be satisfied with enough.

No Perfect People

We may have spent much time and energy looking for perfect people to fulfill our lives. This process involves projecting our fond illusions onto those we meet, building them up way out of reality, and then being terribly disillusioned when extended and intimate acquaintance proves them to be just ordinary people.

Accepting our friends and family for what they are rather than what we idealize them to be, is part of growing up emotionally. It is our own weakness and insecurity that causes us to try to make gods out of other people. As we learn to accept ourselves as less than perfect, we are able to reduce the unreasonable demands we make on others. As we come to know our Higher Power, we do not need to make gods out of fellow human beings.

By not expecting perfection from others, we can love them as they are, encouraging their strengths and supporting their weaknesses.

I pray for the emotional maturity to accept myself and those I love.

Pain

Living without the narcotic of excess food means learning to cope with emotional pain. Uncomfortable feelings which we have covered up by eating begin to surface as we abstain. At first, our emotional reactions are often vague and diffuse, since we have not yet acquired enough insight to identify what it is that is bothering us.

If we are willing to stay with the emotional discomfort and pain, we will eventually gain understanding. Sometimes we have to spend time hurting before we are able to pass through one phase in our development and move on to the next. Whatever the suffering, it is preferable to the agony of a binge. Facing emotional pain is constructive; trying to bury it under food is destructive.

Our pain is often associated with events in the past which are still troubling us unconsciously. When we are able to identify the source of the pain, we can examine it in the light of our present maturity and begin to put it behind us. As long as we avoid feeling the pain, we deny ourselves the healing which our Higher Power can give us.

May I accept the pain which is necessary for continued growth.

Food Is Not Mother

In the mind of a baby, food is synonymous with mother. As the baby grows, the two concepts become differentiated, but perhaps never completely separated. We compulsive overeaters may still be confusing food with mother.

Often we feel a great deal of hostility and resentment toward our mother—she did not give us enough love, or she gave us the wrong kind; she over-fed us, or she denied us what we needed. We may still be searching the refrigerator for the perfect mother! Isn't it about time to realize that she is not there?

No matter what we eat, or how much, we cannot turn back the clock and again become part of our mother. Perhaps instead of being inadequate, our mother was such a great source of comfort and satisfaction that we do not want to face life without a substitute for her presence. Our Higher Power intends that we come to depend on Him even more than we once depended on our mother. He daily offers us a relationship of even greater love and closeness than the one between mother and child. To grow in that relationship requires abstinence from compulsive overeating.

I turn over to You my relationship with my mother.

Cleaning Up

Cleaning up after a meal and taking care of leftovers is a hard job for most compulsive overeaters. What makes it so difficult is our old habit of putting the leftovers in our mouths instead of in the refrigerator or the garbage. Once we decide that we will have nothing at all after our measured meal, the clean-up job becomes amazingly easy.

If we are not spending our energy fighting the temptation to have a bite of this or that, the energy is available for the task that needs to be done. Cleaning up is accomplished with much less time and effort when we are not arguing with ourselves about what happens to the leftovers.

In the past, we may have felt that cleaning up was a demeaning job. As we work our program, we begin to get more satisfaction from all the work we do, and we are less concerned about the relative status of the jobs that fall to us. There is satisfaction in cleaning up after a meal, just as there is satisfaction in cleaning up our lives by means of the OA program.

May I not be too proud to enjoy cleaning up.

Where's the Party?

Most of us have early memories of birthday parties—our own and those of other children—and as compulsive overeaters, we probably remember the food more than anything else. For as long as we can recollect, parties have meant eating and drinking. The better and more abundant the food and drink, the better the party; or so we thought.

Maintaining abstinence means that we will attend parties where we do not eat and drink, if what is available is not on our food plan. In order to do this with serenity and enjoyment, we need to redefine our idea of a party. It is no celebration if we break our abstinence and go back to compulsive overeating.

Through this program, we come to see that a party is something more than an occasion for eating and drinking. Enjoying ourselves with other people requires good will, mutual attraction, and the effort to communicate with and affirm each other. If these elements are present, there will be a party whether or not there is anything to eat or drink. If these elements are absent, no amount of refreshments will ensure a good time.

Thank You for fun.

Plan Plans, Not Results

Understanding that we do not have the power to control the results of our plans is an important step toward accepting reality. We do make plans, based on the information, experience, and insight which we have available to us. The outcome of our plans, however, is dependent on circumstances which are frequently beyond our control.

When we accept the fact that the results of our plans are always in the hands of our Higher Power, we can relax and leave the outcome to Him. When we do not insist compulsively that life go according to our design, we are able to avoid the inevitable frustration produced by such an unrealistic attitude. However good our intentions, our designs are always finite and based on limited knowledge. We need to trust a Power greater than ourselves.

Our idea of what is best for ourselves and those who love may not always be right, according to God's will. The faith that He will carry out His design for us, even when we do not understand it, relieves us of much anxiety and frustration.

I leave results to You.

Asking Directions

When we do not know which way to turn, let us not be too proud to ask for directions. We have found our way to a program which can guide us out of the confusion of compulsive overeating into an ordered, satisfying way of life. In OA, there are people who can give us the directions we need, if we will ask for help.

There is much that we can do on our own— thoroughly studying the literature, planning our three meals a day, establishing firm contact with our Higher Power. When we hit a snag, however, or are unsure of how to handle a difficult situation, we need to promptly seek the assistance our group provides. In order to receive help, we usually need to ask for it.

The illusion that we knew how to manage our lives and did not have to follow anyone else's directions was one of the causes of our difficulties with food and with life in general. Admitting that by ourselves we are powerless enables us to ask for the directions we need.

I ask for Your directions, Lord.

Don't Anticipate

We wear ourselves out unnecessarily when we spend our energy anticipating the future rather than living in the present. To anticipate bad things is obviously detrimental to our serenity. It is also needless, since most of the things we worry about never happen. Even if some of them do occur, it is easier by far to deal with real disasters than with imagined ones.

Anticipating future satisfactions can also be detrimental to our serenity. If we are living for an event or condition which is yet to come, we are not completely alive to what is here now. We may build up some future pleasure in our minds to such an unrealistic pitch that the actual event is bound to be disappointing.

Accepting the here and now is what ensures our sanity and our serenity. Reality is never more than we can manage, with the help of our Higher Power. It is our anticipation of the future which is unreal and dangerous.

May I live today and leave the future to You.

Pinpointing Anxiety

Many of us suffer from a vague, nameless anxiety for which we are unable to find a source. We do not know exactly what we fear, but we know that we are afraid. In the past, we tried to dispel this ominous anxiety by eating.

As long as we overate compulsively, we made it more difficult to get at the reasons for our anxiety. Trying to cover it up with food did not get rid of it, and until we stopped eating compulsively we were unable to identify the source of our anxiety.

By abstaining, we face anxiety rather than trying to cover it up. If we are willing to put up with a certain amount of emotional discomfort, we will be able to understand and work through many of the irrational notions that have made us anxious. Our Higher Power allows buried fears to surface as we acquire the strength and faith to confront them. When we are abstinent, we are able to define our anxiety more clearly and handle it with greater maturity.

By Your light, may we see our irrational anxiety for what it is.

Waking Up To Truth

Our illusions were tied to our compulsive overeating behavior. Abstaining from the behavior makes it possible for us to let go of our illusions. It is the Higher Power that leads us into the truth which penetrates and dispels illusions.

Working the Steps, reading the OA literature, and talking with other members prepares us to receive new truth. Our Higher Power gives us insights, sometimes in quick flashes of perception and sometimes slowly over a long period of time. The experience of discovery is one of the most rewarding facets of our program. It is an on-going process, since we continue to grow and become aware of new truth.

Too much food kept us in a fog. Now we are recovering from the physical effects of our addiction to refined sugars and carbohydrates and the emotional dependency on eating to avoid feeling pain. In the process, we wake up to more and more truth about ourselves, others, and our Higher Power.

May I live by the truth that You reveal.

Loving Truth

Since it is truth that sets us free—free from our addiction and free from crippling fear—we come to love this truth, even when it hurts. It was mainly our fear that kept us from recognizing the truth about ourselves. We needed help and support from a Higher Power before we could face reality. Now that we are sustained by the OA program, we can devote our time and energy to striving for truth in all that we think, say, and do.

Our devotion to truth may bring us into conflict with those around us. What we need to remember is that we are not responsible for convincing anyone else of what we believe to be true. We are honest about where we are, but we do not expect or demand agreement from anyone else. Since each of us has a different perspective, we can only know the truth as we each understand it. Loving truth means that we acknowledge it to be too big for any one of us to grasp completely.

Increase my devotion to Your truth.

Alive To Truth

Being alive to truth requires being in touch with ourselves and with our Higher Power. It requires that we value spiritual truth more than material things. We come to realize that the insights and emotional growth we gain through this program are more valuable than the things we used to think we had to have.

Being alive to truth involves living each present moment. If we are obsessed with the past or preoccupied with the future, we will miss the truth of now. Today we can be who we are and give of our best in whatever situation we find ourselves.

Our Higher Power promises that if we ask for truth, we shall receive it. It will be found when we seek it more than status, money, or physical comfort. When we are alive to truth, we are open to the source of Power which will never let us down.

Today, I will be alive to truth.

Escape Into Sleep

After we stop eating compulsively, we may be tempted to use sleep as a form of escape. Though not as detrimental as excess food, too much sleep can also make us lethargic and dull. The danger lies in allowing ourselves to escape the realities of living, rather than coping with them.

We all need adequate rest in order to feel good and function efficiently. Sleep becomes an escape, however, if we take long daytime naps instead of finding worthwhile and enjoyable activities. Just as we may have overeaten because of boredom, we may oversleep because we have nothing better to do.

Our Higher Power has a plan for the time and talents He gives us. It is our job to discover how and where we can best serve God and each other. With the new life we are given in OA goes the responsibility to use it productively. Since this is the only life we have, we do not choose to sleep it away. By facing our problems with the help of this program, we learn how to deal with them.

Deliver me from indolence.

No Exit

We have tried many ways of avoiding problems and pain. In addition to food, we may have used alcohol, drugs, sleep, sex, compulsive activity, or excessive daydreaming to try to escape whatever it was that we did not want to encounter. Undoubtedly, we found that nothing worked permanently; the problem or pain remained.

It is the attempt to avoid discomfort that turns fear into panic. Whatever troubles or threatens us becomes more unmanageable when we pretend that it does not exist. Now that we have the OA program and contact with a Power greater than ourselves, we can confront our problems without searching frantically for an exit from reality.

Our pain is what teaches us the things we need to know. By being willing to be broken, we are able to become whole. Through our distress, we are watched over by the One who heals us. We need no exit.

Thank You for the faith that overcomes panic.

Appetite Is Not Hunger

Confusing a "hearty" appetite with genuine, physical hunger is a mistake made consistently by compulsive overeaters. Our idea of how much food our body needs is usually a great exaggeration of the actual requirement. Because of an overdeveloped appetite, we are unfamiliar with the feeling of true hunger.

Since we cannot rely on subjective feelings to tell us how much we need to eat, we require an objective, definite plan. When we reach our normal weight, we continue to eat according to a measured food plan, rather than according to appetite. We will never to able to satisfy the demands of our appetite without destroying ourselves physically, emotionally, and spiritually.

When we think we require more food than is called for by our plan, we need to examine our thinking. Usually we find that we are being deluded by the demands of our overdeveloped appetite. We would *like* to eat more, but in fact, our body does not *need* more.

I pray for the wisdom to distinguish between appetite and hunger.

Eating For Mother

As babies and children, we made Mother happy by eating what she gave us. Since our emotions were closely tied to hers, when she was happy, we were also happy. We may have developed the mistaken notion that the more we ate, the happier Mother would be and, therefore, the happier we would be.

This illusion may be persisting into our adult life. On some level, we may not yet realize that no amount of food we can eat will make Mother permanently happy, anymore than it will make us happy. We may have eaten many times in the past in order to please Mother, rather than because we really wanted the food. Subconsciously, we may still think we could please her by consuming more food than we need.

Working the OA program often brings to light other things we are doing in order to please someone else. Since each individual is responsible for his own happiness, there is nothing we can do to ensure the happiness of another individual. Realizing this on a gut level is a powerful tool for maintaining abstinence.

May I realize the futility of eating to please someone else.

Moods

We used to allow our moods to determine what and how much we ate. If we were feeling good, charged up with enthusiasm, we were usually able to focus our energy on some activity other than eating. Perhaps being in a particularly good mood made it possible for us to stick to some kind of diet for a few days.

When the bad moods struck, we invariably turned to excess food for consolation, and we attempted to make the bad moods go away by eating to excess. Any sort of psychic distress became a signal for food.

Then, too, some of us found ourselves overeating in times of elation, because we had no other way to express our joy.

When we are committed to abstinence, we have a rock-like foundation for our eating habits which no shifting mood can destroy. No matter how we may feel at a given moment, we abstain from eating compulsively. Moods change and pass away, but abstinence remains.

Make firm my commitment to abstinence.

Depression

All of us go through times of depression. When we were overeating, we may have felt depressed almost continually. We find that abstinence and the OA program lift us out of depression. The outward circumstances of life may not change radically, but by means of our program we experience more inner joy and contentment and less gloom and despair.

When we do feel depressed, we can take positive action. We can work on a specific step. We can make a phone call. We can offer to help someone else. Focusing our attention on someone or something outside of ourselves is an effective means of combatting depression.

Maintaining abstinence does not ensure that we will never again feel depressed. In general, however, our spirits do not sink as low as they did before and they do not stay down as long. As we improve our contact with our Higher Power, we find ourselves less and less despondent. We have new hope, faith, and love—all powerful antidotes to depression.

Thank You for lifting me out of depression.

Turning On

Before OA, many of us were in a self-centered rut. We had little enthusiasm for anything except food, and food proved to be a false friend. When we come to OA and admit that we are powerless over food, we can turn on to a Power greater than ourselves.

Just as we do not need to understand the complexities of electricity in order to benefit from it, we do not need to understand everything about God in order to receive His power. Taking the Twelve Steps turns us on to a new way of life, motivated by faith in a Higher Power.

Turning on to this Power means that we are no longer alone. We do not have to try to run our lives by ourselves. God can and will relieve us of our obsession with food and our obsession with self. He gives us hope and strength and enthusiasm for the living of our daily lives. Through surrender, we become recipients of the Power of the universe.

Take away the blindness which prevents us from turning on to Your power.

Principles Before Personalities

One of the strengths of our fellowship lies in the fact that we place principles before personalities. OA is not a social club. We form meaningful and lasting friendships, but personal friendship is always subordinate to the program itself.

Putting principles before personalities means that we may expect help and consideration from any other member. Conversely, we are expected to give our attention and assistance to anyone who asks, regardless of how well we like that individual personally. The Twelve Steps and principles of OA unity are more important than the personal relationships of any members in our group.

Because we are committed to abstinence from compulsive overeating and to working the program, we respond honestly and say what we believe to be in the best interest of those we sponsor and those we talk with. We do no one a favor if we dilute our program in order to make it more palatable to someone we personally like.

May I remember to place principles before personalities.

Regaining Control

Temporary loss of control resulting in a slip does not need to send us off on a protracted binge. We have tools which we may use to regain control and re-establish firm abstinence.

If we find ourselves deviating from our food plan, however slightly, we need to make contact with our sponsor or another OA member. Honestly admitting that we are having trouble prevents us from losing touch with reality and slipping back into our old habits. If we pretend that all is well when it is not, we cut ourselves off from the help and support we need.

When we are tempted, it is a good idea to remove ourselves from the source of temptation and get involved in another activity. Reading the literature and/or going to a meeting can renew our OA commitment.

In the last analysis, it is our Higher Power who provides the control which we lack. To turn over our lack of control is to open ourselves to the Power that keeps us abstinent.

Control my life, Lord.

What Am I Avoiding Now?

If I am becoming preoccupied with thoughts of food and eating, I am probably avoiding something in the present which troubles me. We compulsive overeaters have a long history of using food to avoid facing whatever is bothering us. Abstaining may not solve the problem, but at least we do not eat ourselves into a worse situation.

Sometimes we are aware of a difficult task that needs to be done, and we think we require extra food to fortify ourselves in order to accomplish the task. Remembering that excess food incapacitates rather than strengthens is essential to our recovery. A short-term euphoria is not worth the long-term anguish which inevitably follows loss of control.

We are learning to turn to a Power greater than ourselves when we have problems that we formerly avoided or tried to solve by eating. Whatever our perplexity, God has the answer, if we will surrender our wills and listen for His guidance.

Teach me to trust You completely.

One Bite Means a Binge

By this time, we know that we do not overeat moderately. One extra compulsive bite sooner or later becomes a binge. Keeping this fact firmly planted in our consciousness prevents us from deluding ourselves into disaster. For us, there is abstinence or there is chaos. Nothing in between.

Having proved this fact over and over again, we must avoid at all costs the insanity that makes us think we can handle one small extra bite. Our only sure defense against such inexplicable insanity is a Power greater than ourselves. Alone, we cannot control what we eat and we cannot manage our lives.

Each day we begin by admitting to God our powerlessness over our compulsion, and we ask for His control. Whenever we are tempted or overwhelmed, we release our whole selves into His care and protection. At the end of the day, we give thanks for the Power that keeps us from taking the one small, disastrous bite.

Deliver me from the bite that means a binge.

A Strong Father

Many of us understand God in terms of a father, one on whom we can rely no matter what the situation. Our biological father may have been a tyrant or a pal, remote or accessible, firm or weak. However much we loved him and depended on him, he was only a person and not infallible.

For recovery from compulsive overeating, we need a source of strength to which we may turn in any emergency. We require a Power to lean on through the minor ups and downs of every day. Though our families and friends support us, their assistance is not enough. They can provide neither the control nor the sustenance which we need in order to recover from our illness.

The firm, unfailing guidance which we require comes from our Higher Power. If we are willing to again become as children and cast ourselves on God without reservation, we shall receive His support. It is His Power that frees us from our false dependency on food.

Be for us a strong Father, we pray.

Flexibility

If we examine our behavior patterns when we were eating compulsively, we usually find that they were quite rigid. Our mental obsession and physical addiction kept us bound in repetitive behavior which permitted very little spontaneity. With so much time and energy tied up in eating, we had very little flexibility. Most of our free time was used to support our addiction in one way or another.

As we recover, we may find ourselves threatened by unstructured time or by impromptu changes in schedule. An unexpected holiday can bring on feelings of emptiness or boredom. Changed plans can leave us feeling confused and unsettled. Without a firm routine, we may become uneasy.

Remembering that abstinence is the most important thing in our life without exception can provide an anchor when we are required to be flexible. As long as we remain abstinent, we are free to alter schedules and plans according to preference and convenience. Flexibility and spontaneity are possible when abstinence is firm.

Show me how to be flexible.

Survival

We will never make it if we feel we are responsible for solving everyone else's problems. It is tempting to our ego to feel that we can exercise control over the lives of those around us, but it is counter to reality. We cannot protect those we love from sadness, sickness, or pain. Making martyrs of ourselves only prepares the ground for future retaliation.

Our primary task is to remember our dependence on our Higher Power and by His grace to maintain our abstinence. The problems which we face are best dealt with if our spiritual condition is strong. Without abstinence from compulsive overeating, we are not much help to anyone, least of all ourselves.

There are times when all we can manage is to hang on, to survive. We know in our heads that these times will eventually pass. Practicing Step Eleven convinces us in our hearts that God is in charge, no matter how far away He may seem to be.

By Your grace, may I survive the hard times.

Emotional Distress

In the past, we translated emotional distress into physical hunger. Physical hunger was something we could deal with when emotional pain was too much for us. The reason our hunger was not satisfied by any amount of food was that the hunger was really distressed emotion.

If as children we were unable to recognize and express our distress, we buried it. As adults, we may still have ignored painful feelings and tried to make them go away with quantities of food and drink. Eventually, we became so dishonest with ourselves that we did not know what it was we really felt. We may have pretended for so long that everything was fine that we believed it. The telltale sign that all was not fine was our compulsive overeating behavior.

When we abstain, we sometimes fear that we will be overwhelmed with the emotional pain that is no longer buried with food. By turning this distress over to our Higher Power, we are able to survive it and learn from it.

I give You the pain which I cannot handle.

Guilt

It was often a feeling of guilt which led us to overeat, and the more we overate, the more guilty we felt. A Fourth Step inventory can pin-point the reasons for the guilt that we still experience, and by taking the Fifth Step we are able to express and release this guilt.

Some of our guilt feelings are unnecessary. We may experience a sense of guilt when we say "no" to requests and demands which infringe on our legitimate rights. We may feel guilty when we do not live up to the expectations of someone close to us. We need to develop a strong sense of self-worth so that we do not suffer from guilt at not conforming to someone else's image of who we should be.

Working our program relieves us of unnecessary guilt. When we make amends to those we have in fact injured, we are freed from a heavy burden of real guilt. When we experience confirmation of who we are through contact with our Higher Power, we are liberated from the constraint of imagined guilt.

Show us how to deal with guilt.

Insanity

The longer we maintain abstinence from compulsive overeating, the more we realize how insane we were before we found OA. Our withdrawal from people and reality into eating to excess was definitely not a sane way to live. As we work the Steps of this program, we see that many of our thoughts and attitudes were as insane as our destructive behavior.

It is our Higher Power who restores us to sanity, but He requires our surrender and cooperation. We can actively seek out the people and experiences which are life-enhancing rather than detrimental to our mental, emotional, physical, and spiritual well-being. The activities and associations which went along with our compulsive overeating in the past may have to be eliminated if we are to enjoy a sane, sober life in the present and future.

Continuing to beat our heads against the brick walls of past failures is insanity. We have a new life to live, provided we relinquish the attitudes and behavior which we now know to be insane.

Preserve us from old insanities.

Our Daily Bread

Doing the will of our Higher Power each day is what sustains us. We trust Him to provide the food we need, both physical and spiritual. We do not have to be anxious about our supply for the future. If we seek to do God's will today, He will take care of us in the future as well.

Anxiety over material things arises when we forget to stay in touch with the source of our existence. By ourselves, we cannot even assure an adequate intake of oxygen, much less all of the other elements we need for survival. Since we are dependent on our environment to sustain us, we make life extremely difficult when we try to live a self-centered existence.

Our daily sustenance comes from a Power greater than ourselves. As children of God, we have faith that He will take care of us. Exaggerated emotional dependence on physical food blocks us from the spiritual nourishment which our Higher Power offers us today and every day.

Give us this day our daily bread.

Challenges

When we were overeating compulsively, we accepted few challenges other than how much food we could cram into our stomachs without getting sick. As our disease progressed, outside interests narrowed and we "got by" with minimum accomplishment instead of being inspired to do our best.

Life is a challenge. None of us has an easy, free ride. The problems and difficulties we overcome are what ensure our continual growth. Without obstacles and tension, we would stagnate. By overeating, we kept ourselves too doped up and lethargic to respond to many of the challenges which life presented.

Abstinence is a challenge. It requires our devotion, determination, and dedication. There are some days when maintaining abstinence is all the challenge we can handle. As we progress in the program, we are increasingly capable of responding to the challenges that come to us through our families, jobs, leisure activities, and community involvements.

Today, I will be challenged to become what You intend.

Stretching

If we do only what feels good and what is comfortable, we do not grow. If we do not stretch our minds, we vegetate intellectually. If we do not discipline our bodies, we become physically flabby and weak. If we do not exercise our good will, we stay emotionally immature.

To settle for minimum achievement is to miss the satisfaction of accomplishing more than we once thought possible. It is trite but true that we never know what we can do until we try. Abstaining from all refined sugars and carbohydrates may have seemed impossible to us at one time. Accomplishing this, through the help of our Higher Power and OA, makes possible other achievements that we formerly may have considered to be beyond our reach.

In this program, the only way we can fail is by not continuing to try. By abstaining from compulsive overeating and working the Twelve Steps, we can stretch ourselves to a fuller extent of our physical, mental, emotional, and spiritual potential.

May I not be too lazy to stretch as far as I can.

A Permanent Disability

Compulsive overeating is a permanent disability. We do not look forward to becoming normal eaters at some point in the future. Until we accept the fact that our illness is irreversible, we do not learn how to control it.

We have all tried innumerable methods of regaining the ability to eat normally and spontaneously. Perhaps the most common delusion was believing that once we were thin enough we would be able to eat whatever and however we pleased. We may have thought that if only we could straighten out our interpersonal relationships and arrange circumstances to suit us, then we would no longer be plagued by compulsive overeating.

When I accept the fact that I am and always will be a compulsive overeater, no matter what my weight or how ideal my situation, I accept reality. I will have to live with this disease and control it, with the help of my Higher Power and OA, for the rest of my life. Abstinence is not a temporary cure for my illness, but a permanent method of control.

May I understand the full extent of my disability.

Decisions About Food

We compulsive overeaters often find it extremely difficult to make decisions about food. We wonder if we are getting enough or too much, if we are eating the right kind of food, if we will be hungry tomorrow. The process of planning our three meals a day can be agonizing if we cannot decide which foods to choose.

Here is where a food sponsor can give us the assistance and support we need. Since someone who has traveled the road before us will be informed of our menus, we can relax and know that our decisions will be checked by an objective listener. As long as the choices we make fall under the food plan which we have determined to follow, they will be good decisions.

Having written down our food plan for the day and having given it to our sponsor, we do not need to make any further decisions about food today. Recognizing that our obsessive worry about food is an illness, we will turn off further deliberations and work our program.

Today I will make only those decisions about food which are necessary to my program.

Developing Our Potential

Abstinence is the key to developing our potential. For years, our illness has probably controlled our life and reduced our ability to function. Since so much of our energy was tied up in the mental obsession with food and the physical effects of overeating, we were unable to develop the talents and abilities we possessed.

Getting in touch with a Higher Power gives us contact with the source of our potential. Our self-centeredness kept us from believing in our capacity to be activated by a Power greater than ourselves. When we see and hear of the results produced by working the OA program, we develop faith in our own buried talents.

When food controlled our lives, we were using only a very small percentage of our actual potential for work, recreation, and relationships with other people. Through abstinence from compulsive overeating, we discover strengths, abilities, and energies we never knew we had!

Direct my efforts, Lord.

One Day At a Time

We can only work this program one day at a time. Tomorrow's abstinence will take care of itself if we are abstinent today. It is when we look too far ahead that we become troubled and lose our confidence. Whatever happens, we can cope with it one day at a time.

Worrying about the possibility of being hungry next week destroys today's serenity. Projecting ourselves into future tasks produces unnecessary tension. Wondering how someone may react to something we may say tomorrow causes needless anxiety and robs us of the here and now.

Our Higher Power is with us now, today. By learning to know Him in the present, we grow in faith that He will be with us in the future. He gives us the strength to maintain our abstinence today, and that is the best thing we can possibly do for ourselves. One day at a time, we walk out of darkness into light.

Thank You for this day.

Setting Realistic Goals

Part of growing up is learning to set realistic goals for ourselves. Our grandiose egos used to dare us into dreaming great dreams which led to feelings of failure when the dreams did not materialize. If we expect the impossible of ourselves, we are bound to be disappointed.

Those of us who come into OA with many pounds to lose need to be realistic about the amount of time we allow for achieving the weight loss. We also need to be realistic about the fact that we may never look like fashion models. If we expect all other problems to vanish upon the attainment of a weight goal, we are not being realistic.

Maintaining abstinence, working the Twelve Steps, and attending meetings regularly keeps us in touch with the reality of our disease. The goals we set for ourselves are determined by where we are in actuality right now. Some of us have farther to go than others. The goals we set should challenge us rather than defeat us before we begin.

Show me the goals that are realistic for me today.

Meal By Meal

We abstain from compulsive overeating day by day and meal by meal. After breakfast, we do not worry about how we will feel at dinner time. After breakfast we know that we have had an abstinent meal and that we can forget about food until it is time for lunch. If we allow ourselves to start thinking about what we will have for the next meal, and the meal after that, etc., etc., we turn on our obsession.

The beauty of abstinence is that it permits us to get from one meal to the next without being constantly preoccupied with food. By abstaining from refined sugars and carbohydrates and our individual binge foods, we no longer have to fight the craving for more. By working the Twelve Steps, we fill our minds with nourishing thoughts which drive out our former obsession with food.

This meal, which I have planned, is the only one that concerns me now. I do not need to think about other meals or other foods. I will enjoy this meal, and then I will walk away from food into the rest of my life.

Keep me abstinent, meal by meal.

Accepting Emptiness

There will always be times when we feel empty—physically empty, emotionally empty, spiritually empty. Before we found our Higher Power, these periods of emptiness terrified us, and we had to try to fill ourselves up with something, whether it was food, noise, other people, work, or something else.

We probably still do not like to feel empty, and yet, through the OA program, we are learning that emptiness can be a good thing. When we are empty of the refined sugars and carbohydrates which poisoned us, we are full of energy. When we are empty of anger and resentment, we have room for positive feelings of love, joy and peace. When we are empty of pride and egotism, God can fill us with His power.

Our Higher Power is not ours to command. There is no way that we can receive instant consolation and gratification. By accepting our periods of emptiness, however, we open ourselves to growth and to the Spirit that fills us according to His purposes.

May I be empty of self so that I may be filled with You.

Open Hands

If our hands are tightly clenched, we cannot receive anything with them. In order to benefit from the OA program, we have to let go of whatever we are hanging on to, open ourselves to the program, and be willing to receive. We open our hands to the hands extended in fellowship by our new friends. We open our minds and hearts to new ideas, new truth, and new feelings.

We cannot receive the new way of life if we are closed and unwilling to change. Much of what we hear at meetings may sound strange in the beginning, but if we are receptive, it gradually makes sense. There is nothing about this program which is impossible for any one of us. All that is required is the desire to stop eating compulsively and the willingness to learn how.

If we are having trouble with abstinence, it may be because we are hanging on to old ways and have closed our hands, refusing to take certain parts of the program. Our Higher Power extends to us the tools of recovery through the OA program. All we have to do is open our hands, firmly grasp these tools, and use them.

I open my hands to receive Your gifts.

We Are Sick

Until we realize fully that we are sick, we do not begin to recover. As long as we feel that all we need is a good diet and some willpower, we do not understand the nature of our disease. We would have been able to stop eating compulsively long ago if the answer had been willpower and diet.

When we examine the history of our obesity in the light of the OA program, we see that we are in the grip of an incurable illness which gets progressively worse, never better. Once we accept the fact that there is no cure for our disease, we can begin to develop control. Until we recognize the *seriousness* of our illness, we do not succeed in controlling it.

By acknowledging that our very life depends on maintaining abstinence and practicing the OA principles, we come to terms with the reality of our situation. We can live satisfying, full, rewarding lives if we do not forget that we are sick and that our recovery will never be complete.

Each day, may I not forget that I am sick.

Getting Well

Our recovery is always in process; it is never completed. If we think for a minute that we have conquered our disease and no longer have to consider it, that is the time when we are in danger of slipping. Getting well is what we will be doing for the rest of our lives. Fortunately, we have guidelines and a fellowship to support us.

We are not required to think about our disease twenty-four hours a day. We do need to remember it when thoughts of food and eating arise. We also need to remember it when we find ourselves thinking the kind of thoughts or feeling the moods which led to binges in the past.

Getting well is an adventure. We have moved out of the repetitious rut of past habits and are reaching into the unknown. There are times when we are anxious and fearful that we will not be able to make it. We are not alone. There is a Higher Power that guides us and an organization of friends who sustain us. The process of getting well is a privilege and a gift.

Thank You for the process of getting well.

Remembering

We remember what we were like before we joined OA. We remember the confusion and despair which threatened to overwhelm us. We remember the agony of eating binges which started so innocently and which ended in such pain.

As we recover from compulsive overeating, we remember events from the past in a new light. We see how our disease contributed to seemingly unrelated problems. We recognize feelings which we were not aware of at the time. We understand the real reasons for some of our strange actions and mysterious fears.

At the same time that it keeps us anchored in the present, abstinence helps us to understand the past. Integrating our memories gives us strength and confidence for the future. What we always need to remember is that we are compulsive overeaters still, no matter how long we have abstained. Remembering this fact protects us from allowing our disease to become active again.

Today, I remember that I am a compulsive overeater.

Concentrating

Our program requires concentration. It is not something that we may consider casually in odd bits of leftover time. Since abstinence is the most important thing in our lives, we devote our best energies to maintaining it. Many of us find that time spent concentrating on our program at the beginning of the day is most fruitful.

These periods of concentration do not need to be long. It is the quality of our attention that counts. A few minutes in the morning spent in contact with our Higher Power can set the tone for the entire day. We touch base with who we are and where we are going. Concentrating brings results.

Whenever thoughts of food and eating interrupt our activities, we can stop for a moment to concentrate on our program. Abstinence is not always foremost in our minds, but it is always there when we are threatened by a return to old thoughts and cravings. Compulsive overeating was concentration on food; abstinence is concentration on recovery.

I pray that You will direct my concentration.

Climbing

Eating compulsively was a downhill skid into despair. Recovering is an uphill climb all the way. It is not easy. The line of least resistance is the habit pattern we have built up over past years. Forming new habits is hard work.

We do not stand still. Either we are climbing up step by step into recovery or we are slipping farther down into disease. Each decision we make to abstain from the first compulsive bite takes us another rung up the ladder to health. Each time we refrain from anger, worry, or false pride, we grow emotionally. In every instance where we are able to turn our will over to our Higher Power, we gain spiritual strength.

The climb is what makes life challenging and exciting. To retreat into food is to give up and lose the satisfaction of having reached a higher point in our journey. Realizing that we are and always will be compulsive overeaters makes us aware of our continual need to climb out of illness into recovery.

We are climbing, with Your aid.

A No-Fault Illness

Formerly, we may have blamed our parents, a disappointment in love, economic insecurity, or a million other factors for our addiction to compulsive overeating. We probably spent much time and energy trying to figure out why we overate.

When we get honest with ourselves, we assume the responsibility for our own actions, instead of trying to shift it somewhere else. Many of us come to believe that we would be compulsive overeaters no matter what the circumstances of our lives. As we recover, we see that the why of our illness is unanswerable and unimportant. What counts is how we control it.

We do not continue to berate ourselves for having this illness, or consider ourselves physically, morally, or spiritually inferior for having contracted it. Blaming ourselves is as useless as blaming someone else. We accept the fact that through no one's fault we have the disease of compulsive overeating. Then we get on with the business of learning to control this illness with the help of our Higher Power and the OA program.

I blame no one for my illness.

Paradoxes

Our program contains some surprising paradoxes. When we admit that we are powerless, we can receive Power. When we accept what we do not like, it begins to change. As long as we remember we are sick, we can continue to recover.

The key to these paradoxes is our willingness to believe in a Higher Power. By ourselves, we are weak, ineffectual, and sick. When operating in accordance with the will of the Power greater than ourselves, our potential is limitless.

Until we admit defeat, we will not succeed with the OA program. The biggest defeat is the one that is dealt to our illusions of self-reliance and self-sufficiency. As long as we insist on trying to control our lives by ourselves, we will be confused. It is by relinquishing control that we gain strength and are freed from our compulsion and obsession. We save our lives by giving them away.

May I accept the paradoxes which I do not understand.

Daring

What is it inside our heads that keeps daring us to try once more to prove that we are not compulsive overeaters? What kind of stupidity makes us think that this time we can get away with taking one compulsive bite? In a moment of blind bravado, we can lose months or years of hard-won control.

Our ego is our own worst enemy. We forget that once a compulsive overeater, always a compulsive overeater. We tell ourselves that since we have been doing so well for so long, surely we can manage one or two small deviations. We rebel against the program and place ourselves above it. We forget that we have a disease, and we decide to do what we feel like doing, oblivious to the fact that by taking that first compulsive bite we are destroying our sanity and our serenity.

This kind of daring is to be avoided at all costs. The best antidote is the humility which reminds us of the reality of our illness. We are not like everyone else. We are compulsive overeaters and do not dare to throw away our program.

Save me from the kind of daring which destroys me.

Warning: Danger Ahead

After we have lived the OA program for a time, it becomes a part of our deepest self. When a thought or impulse arises which threatens our program, we often feel a twinge of fear at the same time. This feeling of fear is a warning that whatever we are contemplating may be hazardous to our health.

Not to heed these warning signals is the height of folly. We have learned from sad experience that certain thoughts and actions are not for us, if we want to maintain our abstinence and our sanity. When confronted with a difficult choice, we need to listen carefully for the small voice of conscience which warns us of disaster ahead if we choose foolishly.

Our Higher Power never allows us to be tempted beyond our ability to withstand the temptation, provided we recognize our need for His saving strength. By paying attention to the small warning twinges of fear, we can avoid thoughts and action which go against His will for us.

May I heed the danger signals which You send.

Thinking Straight

Before we found this program, we did a great deal of thinking in circles. Since we did not know how to stop eating compulsively, we spent a lot of time thinking up reasons for our behavior, making plans for change, and rationalizing another day's failure to eat normally. Our thinking often wandered away into fantasy, spinning dreams of when we would be thin and on top of things. Since we had to have reasons for our inability to make the dreams materialize, we blamed our failure on the people around us. If *they* were only more loving, considerate, capable, exciting, smarter . . .

Such circular thinking got us nowhere. The more we fantasized, the more we ate, and the more we ate, the more we withdrew from reality.

When our minds are not muddled by too much food, our thinking is clarified. The Twelve Steps put us on the road to responsible action, rather than irresponsible rationalization. Accepting the fact that we have a disease keeps us in the world of reality instead of a fantasyland.

With Your truth, keep my thinking straight.

Confidence

Our biggest problem was the inability to stop eating compulsively and the resultant obesity. This problem is never solved permanently, but it is overcome on a day-to-day basis. As we succeed in abstaining from compulsive overeating, we grow in confidence. Since by working the program we solve our biggest problem every day, we become confident that we can solve other problems as well.

Confidence is trust that our Higher Power and OA will not let us down. Confidence is the knowledge that however tough life gets, we have tools and resources for dealing with it. Confidence is believing in ourselves as children of God and people of value. Confidence is the willingness to give what we have, with the faith that our gifts are needed and acceptable.

When we have confidence in our Higher Power and in ourselves, we are willing to try even though we may fail. If we fail, we are willing to try again. Since our will and our lives are turned over to God as we understand Him, we have confidence that everything eventually works out for good.

You are the source of confidence.

Control

Control was something we either feared or did not know much about before we began the OA program. We resisted control as being opposed to our idea of spontaneous living, especially spontaneous eating. Control was for other people—our children perhaps—but not for us.

Without control, we watched as self-will ran riot with our lives. We ate what we pleased, and then, angry and depressed, we said what we pleased and did what we pleased. The problem was that we ended up being not at all "pleased," but full of disgust and despair. Dimly, we may have realized that our suffering was due to lack of self-control, but we did not know how to go about acquiring what we lacked.

By relinquishing our so-called control to a Higher Power, we learn what it means to be free. By using the OA concept of abstinence to control our eating, we find spontaneity in living. Rather than inhibiting us, the kind of control we develop through this program liberates us from the bondage of self-will.

Control my life, I pray.

Courage

We pray for the courage to change the things we can. We cannot change the fact that we are compulsive overeaters, but we can change our actions so that we are not destroyed by our disease. Making changes requires the courage to start out on a new, unknown course. Courage does not mean the elimination of fear. Courage means acting in spite of the fact that we are afraid.

It takes courage to learn to affirm one's rights as an individual, especially if the old way was to say "yes" to all demands and requests, reasonable and unreasonable. It takes courage to face the truth instead of continuing to live with comfortable illusions. Courage is necessary for working the steps of the OA program.

Sometimes courage comes when we are pressed to a wall of failure. There is nothing to do but turn around and step out in a new direction, even though we are afraid. The courage born of desperation can produce remarkable results.

Grant us the courage to move in Your direction.

Minimizing Temptation

There are things we can do to minimize the temptations that are around us. We are constantly exposed to food advertisements if we watch television and read magazines. Most of us need to spend a certain amount of time purchasing and preparing food. Social gatherings usually involve refreshments. All of this exposure to food can be uncomfortable for compulsive overeaters if we do not find ways to minimize it.

It is a good idea to skip the recipe sections in the magazines we read. Unnecessary thinking about food only intensifies our obsession. Moving away from the television set during a food commercial is a way to minimize that kind of temptation. Grocery shopping is expedited by not considering any items other than those on a prepared list and by spending as little time as possible in the grocery store. Meal preparation can be simplified so that less rather than more time is spent in the kitchen. At parties, we can concentrate on people and conversation instead of food.

The best way to handle temptation is by remembering that we are compulsive overeaters and that nothing is worth activating our disease.

Guide us as we avoid temptation.

Working Compulsively

We do not want to turn from compulsive overeating to compulsive working. This, too, is an attempt to escape reality. Compulsive working holds a particular danger for us, since when we allow ourselves to get overtired, we run the risk of breaking our abstinence.

Working compulsively includes the fear that what we do will not be good enough. It is when we are unsure of our self-worth that we have to continually prove how much we can accomplish. Compulsive work is also a way to avoid meaningful relationships with family and friends. If we fear intimacy and exposure, we sometimes try to hide behind a facade of busyness.

When God controls our will and our lives, we work according to His direction. We have the faith that what we do will be acceptable and enough. Believing that God cares for us, we do not rely only on our own abilities. Working for a Higher Power means that we work with serenity and confidence, knowing that He directs and sustains our efforts.

Teach me how to work productively for You.

Fear of Failure

It is often the fear of failure which prevents us from attempting what we really want to do. When we are new to OA, we may be reluctant to commit ourselves to abstinence because we fear we will break it. When we are able to maintain abstinence from compulsive overeating, we may be afraid to make some other kind of commitment for fear of not being able to succeed.

Our past failures can undermine our confidence in our present abilities. For this reason, we need to let go of the past and be willing to try something new. For many of us, belief in a Higher Power is a new commitment. The fear that we will be disappointed sometimes blocks us from the wholehearted trust that such a commitment entails.

The fear of failure is best dealt with by living one day at a time. We can risk a small failure today; it is the large failure in the future that terrifies us. By taking a small step today toward maintaining abstinence or working on an important project, we build the confidence that we can eventually succeed.

With Your support, may I be willing to risk failure.

No Exceptions

Abstinence is the most important thing in my life without exception. Since I am a compulsive overeater, any exception would mean that I might lose control. If I do not control my disease, it controls me. Therefore, there are no exceptions to the rule that abstinence is the most important thing in my life.

In order to follow this rule, I need to depend on a Power greater than myself. Alone, I am not strong enough to maintain abstinence at all times and in all places, but through the grace of God and the support of the OA fellowship, I can do it.

With abstinence, the rest of my life falls into place. I have an incurable illness, but one which can be controlled day by day through following the OA program, working the Twelve Steps, and staying in contact with my Higher Power. There are good days and bad days, but there is always abstinence. I am grateful to be an abstaining, recovering, compulsive overeater.

May I remember each day that there are no exceptions to abstinence.